PARENTING: AN HEIR-RAISING EXPERIENCE

PARENTING:
AN
HEIR-RAISING EXPERIENCE

Raising Your Child
With Confidence

Mary Glynn Peeples
and
Dr. Sam Peeples, Jr.

THE SHEEP SHOPPE
P.O. BOX 531147
BIRMINGHAM, ALABAMA 35253
(205) 871-0380

Parenting:
An Heir-Raising Experience
Raising Your Child With Confidence

Copyright © 1994 by Mary Glynn Peeples and Dr. Sam Peeples, Jr.

Published by The Sheep Shoppe
    P.O. Box 531147
    Birmingham, Alabama 35253

Illustrator: Patt DeFrieze
Editor: Betsy Lee

Library of Congress Catalogue Card Number: 93-086760

First Printing, 1994
Printed in the United States of America

ISBN 0-9634836-1-7

To our grandchildren
Mark, Sam, Gil and Lauren
who have brought great
joy into our lives.

Acknowledgment

We owe a debt of gratitude to those who were so generous with their time and expertise;

Dr. Henry Brandt who has always been there for us when we needed him. When we think of Henry the word "wisdom" comes to mind. Many days we wondered how the children would turn out or if we would hold out! Dr. Brandt's words ring in my ear, "Don't loose the ball in the last quarter!" We could always trust his advice because he backed it up with the truth, a Bible verse!

Betsy Lee who tirelessly and patiently edited our manuscript and made it reader friendly! Betsy gave us creative ways to state many of our thoughts.

Patt DeFriese who has added color and humor to many pages. She has helped to make the stories memorable with her captivating illustrations.

Contents

Introduction

Habits become patterns that we use in performing certain functions. Many of these functions are performed on such a routine basis that we are not conscious of what we are doing. The behavior and attitude of the child often dictates the method the parent uses in raising the child. The very thought that the method could be incorrect never seems to cross our mind. It didn't in ours. Instead counsel is sought in how to get the child to behave differently in an environment where the wrong methods are being practiced. And coupled with this, efforts are made or counsel is sought in how to improve the wrong methods!

Could it be there are different methods? And that these different methods could be better? In this book we want to present some different methods of parenting. These methods are based upon biblical principles. We are strongly convinced that these methods, while different, have proven to be better. These convictions have developed from two sources. One, using them in our own home for two generations, (children and grandchildren) and secondly, working with scores of parents over the last 15 years who have sought our counsel.

The greatest obstacle to overcome — change. We believe that change is the most difficult task that people ever face. To enable you to accomplish this difficult task we want to present several different and yes, better methods of parenting. To convince you of their authenticity and to motivate you to practice them, we will relate many stories from our own family and those who sought our help.

We became Christians in our mid thirties and were very unfamiliar with the Bible. As we began to read, study, and attend conferences, we were amazed at the practical information the Bible contains regarding parenting.

Many of the verses we found are the basis for the principles used in each chapter. Our goal is to share with you a few general principles which have broad application. As you consider their application don't succumb to the temptation that your child or your situation is an exception.

As you trouble shoot problems with your child we suggest you follow this principle. "Whenever you are experiencing a *specific* problem, you have violated a *general* principle." Learn to identify the general principle and use it to solve the specific problem. If you will do this on a consistent basis, you will reduce the possibility of repeated recurrences of the problem. Simply dealing with the problem over and over without factoring in the general principle will guarantee its repetition.

We desire that you benefit from the information provided by our creator in carrying out your parenting responsibilities. It is often said:

FOR BEST RESULTS FOLLOW THE INSTRUCTIONS OF THE MAKER!

IF ONLY THEY CAME WITH A MANUAL

THEY DO!

CHAPTER 1
GETTING
IN SHAPE
FOR
PARENTING

CHAPTER I

Getting In Shape for Parenting

"Only take heed to thyself, and keep thy soul diligently lest thou forget the things which thine eyes have seen, and lest they depart from thy heart all the days of thy life: but teach them to thy sons, and thy sons' sons."

Deuteronomy 4:9 (KJV)

We built our house on an acre of land. Tall pine trees, a thirty-mile view of the mountains. A quiet woodland stream flowed across the back of the property.

Our major request of the architect was plenty of glass on the back of the house. No one could possibly see inside from that angle. We wanted as much glass as possible. He did a job for us! Each room had sliding glass doors and solid glass panes — our dream house come true. I could sit down and watch the children play without having to get out of my chair!

We had three children in thirty-four months. They were four, five and six years old the year we built the house. Our children never colored or even watched television. They ran through the house, chasing each other, and loved the outdoors, especially playing in the stream.

As a frantic mom, I was always afraid something would happen to my children so I constantly checked on them. I loved to read and knit and resented having to put down my book or needle and yarn to keep track of them in the backyard. The new house with its large glass windows was supposed to solve our problems. Now I could look up and see the children easily without having to stop my activities. No more loosing my place in the book or dropping a stitch on my sweater!

One afternoon I was preparing dinner and the children were playing in our backyard stream. Sam came home from the office. As I heard Sam drive into the garage, the rice boiled over on the stove and the telephone rang.

Our new stove was a mess! Grabbing the handle of the pot, I sat it on the counter and ran for the telephone. As I reached the telephone, I saw three little noses peering through the sliding glass doors. The children had heard Dad come home and ran to greet him.

Each of them had two hands full of mud and a runny nose. I watched red clay run down the glass as muddy hands and runny noses were pressed against the shiny window panes.

Taking one look at the children, I screamed as loud as possible, "Get off that window!" Then I picked up the telephone and answered very politely, "Hello."

My friend asked, "Mary Glynn, are you busy?"

"Why, no," I answered. The tone of my voice was as gentle as a lamb. Covering the mouthpiece of the telephone, I turned to Sam as he walked up the steps. "Get them off that window while I talk on the telephone."

Sam had done nothing. He simply had come home from work. He was even thrilled to be coming home! He hardly knew what to think with all the screaming and confusion as he walked into in his "dream house" that day.

Who Are You Trying to Impress?

I don't remember anything else about the conversation with my friend. I suddenly wished the floor would open so that I could drop into a hole and vanish from sight. I looked at Sam — the man I had pledged my life to, the man I changed my name for, this precious man whom I loved so much.

Then I looked into my five-year-old daughter's eyes. Blond curls covered Dawn's head; her big brown eyes always had a sparkle to them. A real little beauty. Our two boys gazed through the window. Handsome, intelligent little guys.

I realized that I cared much more about what my friends thought of me than what my own family thought. I could scream at my family, but when I spoke with a friend, I became an entirely different person.

I treated the most important man in my life worse than anyone. I treated the three children I had given birth to worse than the puppy running around the yard.

I wondered if I could recommend my lifestyle to my children. Would I want our little girl to grow up to be like me? Could I ask my boys to find Christian women like me to marry? Would I want their wives to talk to them as I had spoken to their father?

I knew the answer to those questions. Every answer was a big NO! I was ashamed and humiliated by my behavior.

Standing in the new house with the glass wall, I prayed the most important prayer since I had prayed to invite Jesus Christ to come into my life: "Lord, please change me. Please cause me to care more about what my family thinks of me than what my friends think. Don't let me have to change the subject of my conversation, the tone of my voice, or the look on my face when a stranger walks into my house."

I wanted desperately to be the same person at home that I was in public places. Do you have this same desire? There is no place like home to reveal the true spirit of a mom and dad.

Therefore, the number one priority of a parent should be to become spiritually and emotionally strong and to learn how to maintain that strength.

The painful story I have just shared reveals a basic need in the heart of all parents. My children's behavior convicted me of a flaw in my *character*, not a flaw in my *parenting skills*. Trying to improve my parenting skills would not have removed the conviction of my personal sin. I needed to get in shape first, before I could help my children.

Parents ask us eagerly how to improve their parenting skills to change the behavior of their child. But this emphasis leads to a common trap. It emphasizes parenting skills without equipping parents to implement these skills.

We'd like to begin by focusing on you, the parent. This chapter offers practical guidelines to help you get into better condition spiritually and emotionally. We have found in working with moms and dads that this information enables them to be more and more consistent as effective parents.

We all know that consistency is important, but how do you achieve it? We have found there are three major roadblocks to consistency. Learning to recognize and jump over these hurdles will take you a long way down the road to successful parenting.

ROADBLOCK #1: SELFISHNESS
There are three natural tendencies that are roadblocks to consistency. According to the Bible, selfishness is the first roadblock.

Having It Our Way

A simple and clear statement of this is found in Isaiah 53:6, "All we like sheep have gone astray; we have turned every one to his own way; and the Lord hath laid on Him the iniquity of us all" (KJV). This verse begins and ends with the word, "all". It must apply to ALL parents. All parents want to have their way with their children. All children want to have their way with their parents. Wanting your way is not the roadblock. The roadblock occurs from the wrong reaction when you don't get your way.

Our natural tendency is finding and maintaining contentment in our lives by having things go our way. The Bible clearly states that God wants to be our source of contentment. It should not be related to our having our way. What goes on inside of you when your children misbehave? The greatest temptation is to examine our expectations of our children. If these expectations are correct, even biblically correct, we tend to justify our reaction. And yet our internal reaction can be *more* damaging than our children's offensive behavior.

People who repress their emotions believe that reactions not expressed are reactions they can ignore. But even if the reactions occur only on the inside, they still have the same damaging effect as if they were expressed outwardly. It is also a popular belief that by expressing (venting) our reactions we free ourselves of those emotions. This is simply not true. Now the destructive reaction is not only on the inside, but also on the outside.

The most common and damaging reaction is anger. In a later chapter we will deal more completely with this subject. It is easy to deceive yourself. When you're angry inside, but you don't act angry, you tell yourself that you're not angry. Yet you may constantly be involved in a "slow burn" on the inside.

Acting Nice

Once Dr. Henry Brandt, a Christian psychologist and author, was visiting our home. My friend, Jane, came to meet him. We stood on the porch and said our good-bys. As Jane walked to her car, I turned to Henry and said, "Isn't she nice?"

Henry replied, "I don't know if she is nice or not."

This startled me. What a cynical and harsh statement! "Well, she acts nice to me!" I said.

Henry laughed, "I can go along with that. She may *act* nice, but I have no idea if she *is* nice. I can't see inside her heart. Anyone can act nice and not be nice!"

I was critical of Henry, but time proved that he was correct. We have encountered many parents who act nice. But as we come to know them as we deal with their problems, we find that they are deceitful actors.

Sam and I have been guilty of the same thing all too often. For example, on some Sundays we would experience harsh conflict on the way to church. Holding hands, with smiles our faces, we would walk down the aisle and take our seats as if we were the best of friends. We may have fooled the congregation, but we never fooled our children.

Standing in the new house with the glass wall, holding the telephone in one hand, looking at my family, I knew that I was the biggest hypocrite in town. I felt the same way when I walked down that church aisle.

Lord, Change Me

A parent's most important job is to raise children. Home is the most important place a parent goes. If we know our children should be a priority, then why do we so often see them as an interruption? Why do we view them this way? Parents have their plans and children interfere with them. Their behavior and interference reveals our selfishness. A major part of selfishness is wanting to have our own way.

As I looked at the glass with the muddy hand prints, my anger was revealed. I didn't get my way because I didn't want the children to put their dirty hands on the glass. The last thing I wanted to do was to clean those large windows. Now I had to stop what I was doing to clean. The children became an interference in my day.

Remember my prayer, "Lord, change me?" God began by showing me things that needed to be changed in my own life right away. I was a selfish, angry, bitter woman. I was fine until the children got in my way. Family living will reveal the natural tendency to want to have our own way.

God's Provision

God has made provision for this natural tendency. The need to have our way is at the heart of our old nature. It is indeed the *nature* of human nature. In the Old Testament this tendency is often called "iniquity." If you recall, this word is found in our verse, Isaiah 53:6. "All we like sheep have gone astray; we have turned every one to his own way; and the Lord hath laid on Him the iniquity of us all" (KJV). The last half of this verse says that Jesus had to come in order for this singular tendency to be laid upon Him. Iniquity is common to us all. All of our sins (plural) spring from this (singular) source - iniquity. (See Mark 7:21-23 and Galatians 5:19-21).

Christ paid the penalty. Now we need to understand God's provision to meet our daily need. This is clearly found in Galatians 5:16 & 17, "This I say then, Walk in the Spirit, and ye shall not fulfil the lust of the flesh. For the flesh lusteth against the Spirit, and the Spirit against the flesh: and these are contrary the one to the other: so that ye cannot do the things that ye would." (KJV)

This verse teaches us that God's provision for the flesh is the Holy Spirit's control. The flesh does not change nor is it eradicated. It is simply to be controlled *moment by moment* by the Holy Spirit.

Sometimes there is confusion about what it means to "walk in the Spirit." In its simplest terms, it means walking through life with the

Holy Spirit in control. How do you enter into this? You make a total submission to God. Through prayer, you yield your life to Him. You ask Him to be in control.

When the Holy Spirit is in control, one of His jobs is to convict us of sin. As we walk in the Spirit, our awareness of sin increases. This conviction should be followed by confession. "If we (freely) admit that we have sinned and confess our sins," Scripture says, "He is faithful and just (true to His own nature and promises) and will forgive our sins - dismiss our lawlessness - and continuously cleanse us from all unrighteousness - everything not in conformity to His will in purpose, thought and action" I John 1:9 (AMP). The Holy Spirit shows us our sin in order for us to confess and be cleansed and free from it. Once the sin is gone, there is nothing to repress or express. Nothing to hide. No more deceit!

At this point you are clean and empty. It is good to be cleansed from sin, but it isn't good to be empty. Ask to be filled with love, joy, peace and patience. Children need loving, joyful, peaceful, patient parents. As you act or react and sin again, you must repeat these two steps: confess and ask to be filled.

This enables you to experience a consistent walk with the Lord. As you do this, you will see the influence of your lower nature, selfishness, diminish in your life.

ROADBLOCK #2: LOOKING TO OTHERS FOR JOY
The second natural tendency that often becomes a roadblock
to consistency is looking to the creation for love, joy, peace, and
comfort, rather than to the Creator. The "creation" consists of
people, places, things and events. Many times we depend on
these for our emotional stability.

HAS YOUR CHILD'S BEHAVIOR EVER DETERMINED HOW
YOUR DAY GOES?

If you answer yes, you have just given evidence to the effect of this
second natural tendency.

The Big Speech

Once a friend of Sam's asked him to review a speech he was going
to give to his son. The boy had caused great trouble in their family.
His parents had endured terrible pain due to the choices made by this
rebellious child.

The speech began, "Son, you are driving your mother crazy and
your dad can only work until noon each day because his energy level
has expired." Sam interrupted him and asked him to repeat what he
had just said. He did repeat it. Sam then asked him, "Are you announcing to your child that his behavior is determining his mother's mental
health? And are you saying that your energy level is directly related to
your son's behavior?" The friend was startled and stopped short. He
was totally unaware of what he was communicating to his son.

He thought if he made the child aware of his parents' suffering, this
young man would be motivated to change. He also thought the extent
of their suffering would be an indication to the boy of the serious
impact of his wrong behavior.

Sam asked his friend if he felt this was too much responsibility to
place on a child. What a heavy burden for a young person to bear the
responsibility for his parents' emotional stability. Parents have a constant responsibility to train children. This man was a committed Christian. Without realizing what he was doing, he was training his son to
believe that the normal Christian life means looking to others for one's
emotional stability.

Sam had to remind this "committed Christian" that the fruit of the
Spirit is love, joy, peace, and comfort, NOT the fruit of an obedient
child (Galatians 5:22 & 23).

In John 14:27, Jesus says, "Peace I leave with you; My (own) peace I now give *and* bequeath to you. Not as the world gives do I give to you. Do not let your hearts be troubled, neither let it be afraid - stop allowing yourselves to be agitated and disturbed; and do not permit yourselves to be fearful and intimidated and cowardly and unsettled" (AMP). In *The Living Bible* the world's peace is described as being "fragile." The word *fragile* depicts something that is easily broken and cannot withstand pressure or stress.

Sam's friend's experience is an accurate illustration of this truth. When his son's behavior produced stress in the home, his fragile peace broke. The Creator designed us in such a way that we are to get our love, joy, peace and comfort from Him - and from Him *alone*!

Mixtures Make Messes

We often find ourselves trying to make a mixture work. Christians would never leave God out. But because of our strong natural tendency to look to the creation for our emotional stability, we attempt to mix the fruit of the Spirit with an obedient child. We expect this mixture to produce a peace and joy that withstands pressure and stress.

"I have told you these things, that My joy *and* delight may be in you," said Jesus, "and that your joy *and* gladness may be of full measure *and* complete *and* overflowing" John 15:11 (AMP). Years ago Sam found an easy test to evaluate his source of joy. Many times when one of our children misbehaved, Sam lost his joy. Since Jesus said His joy would be full and complete and overflowing, Sam realized that the Lord was not his source of joy.

When our son Mark was twenty-one, he had a factory job. One morning at 7:45 Sam went to Mark's room to try to get him out of bed. He was due to be at work at 8:00. Mark rolled over in bed. His boss was out of town and wouldn't even know if he was late to work, Mark told his dad. Sam was furious. He lashed out at Mark, "It makes no difference who's on the job. Your responsibility is to be there on time. Get up and go to work!"

Mark did as he was told. He slammed the front door and left in a hurry. I was shattered by the scene. I waited for enough time to lapse for Mark to arrive at his job, then I called him to be sure he went to work. Mark told me he wasn't coming home. He was sick of his dad talking to him in such an angry manner.

It was obvious to all of us that Sam had lost his joy. He was a very angry father. Sam justified his anger because of Mark's slothful behavior. Because Mark's behavior was wrong it made it easy for Sam to justify his sinful response.

Later that morning Sam asked the Lord to forgive him for his anger and to restore his joy. He called Mark on the telephone and apologized for his harshness.

Mark finished work at 5:00. I was waiting at the front door to see his car drive in the driveway. What a thrill to see Mark come home. Apparently his dad's apology was enough for Mark. He never mentioned the scene. We don't know what was going on in Mark's heart, but we know about Sam's heart.

When parents right their wrongs, the proper environment in the home is restored. This kind of environment seems to make it easier for children to get on with their life. This is also the best way for a parent to teach a child how to right his own wrongs.

Slavery

It is easy for parents to become their children's slaves. This happens when we make them our source of joy and peace. One of the best definitions of slavery is, "When my mental health is being determined by someone else's behavior." The Apostle Peter documented this truth when he said, "for of whom a man is overcome, of the same is he brought in bondage" II Peter 2:19 (KJV).

If Sam had continued to be angry with Mark instead of confessing his sin and asking the Lord to restore his joy, he would have become Mark's slave.

We need to be constantly aware of how these natural tendencies affect us and our responsibilities as parents. Parents should have an ongoing prayer for the Lord to make them aware of their stubborn insistence to have their way and of their response when things don't go their way — especially when the parent's way is right, which makes it easy to justify a sinful response.

LOOK TO THE LORD FOR YOUR SOURCE OF JOY AND PEACE, NOT YOUR CHILDREN. If you look to your children for your emotional stability, then when you become emotionally unstable, your natural response will be to blame them.

ROADBLOCK #3: BLAMING OTHERS
The third natural tendency that can be a roadblock to consistency is blaming others for our emotional instability instead of taking responsibility for our actions and reactions. This roadblock is the most difficult to recognize. The tendency to blame someone else is so ingrained in our thinking it is difficult to think otherwise!

All of us would agree that it's important to take personal responsibility for our behavior. In order to better understand this, Sam sums it up this way:

> *The circumstances of life,*
> *The events of life,*
> *The people around me in life,*
> *Do not make me the way I am,*
> *but reveal the way I am.*

When most parents hear this, they see themselves as the exception to the rule. How could this apply to their family? The truth is that our children never make us angry. They reveal the anger in us that is already there. When Sam and I suggest this to parents, their typical response is: "How can you say this when you've never met MY child? I guess I didn't know that's what you meant. I'll have to think about this."

We reply, "What does our knowing your child have to do with whether or not this is true?" It's easy for us to understand these parents' point of view. There have been many times in our experience when we've made our situation an exception. I can vividly recall one of these times in my life.

Righting A Wrong

When Dawn was six, I bought her a beautiful blue dress with lace and appliqued animals across the front. She loved this dress and looked lovely in it. It was her "Sunday special." Dawn wanted in the worst way to wear the dress to school so her friends could see it.

She begged and pleaded with me to let her wear it just one time. She made many promises if I would give in to her pleading and allow her to show off the dress to her first grade class. She promised not to get it dirty. She promised to be extra careful. "Please Mom, let me wear it just one day." The answer was always NO!

One morning the car pool horn sounded. The station wagon with a mom and four children had come to pick up our three. The car waited in the driveway, motor running. Time to go! Sam and Mark ran through the den, gave me a kiss, grabbed their lunch boxes and books. Out the door they ran. I waited for Dawn. She came seconds later with her lunch box and her books in hand, racing to get out the door before I could stop her.

You guessed it! She had on the blue dress with the lace and appliqued animals on the front! I couldn't believe what she'd done. She thought if she had to change her dress, the entire car pool would be late for school. Dawn assumed that I would never cause seven children to be tardy.

She was wrong. I am a Christian, and I'm committed to raising obedient children. She wasn't going to get away with that little trick. "Stop!" I screamed. I grabbed Dawn by the arm, unbuttoned the dress, jerked it over her head and sent her back to her room to find another dress.

I shouted at her as she ran to her room, "You are not going to get by with this. You will do as I say and if all the children in the car are late to school, it will be your fault. Don't you ever do this again. You thought you could get your way but I'll show you that you will DO AS I SAY at all cost."

She put on another dress as I continued to scream. I waited at the door to zip up the dress. As she passed me by, I swatted her on the rear, zipped up the dress and told her to get in the car as fast as she could! She looked into my eyes. Her big brown eyes were filled with tears. One large tear trickled down her cheek. Her chin quivered as she ran to the car.

Closing the door, I returned to the kitchen to put away the breakfast dishes. I felt very uncomfortable. In my mind, I was justifying my anger because of her bad behavior. I began to rationalize: "Who wouldn't be angry when a child deliberately disobeys? Sure, she didn't like the way I treated her, but she'd just have to understand. After all, a Christian mother should see that her children obey her, and be strong and stern in her discipline. Certainly this episode will motivate her never to do this again."

All this time I was blaming Dawn for my discomfort. No matter what I said to myself, the feelings of guilt and frustration continued to increase. As I put the laundry in the washing machine, I felt so dirty I wanted to get in with the clothes!

I went into the bathroom to brush my teeth and wash my face. It was now 9:00 in the morning. I was scheduled to speak for an evangelistic coffee at one of my friend's homes. What I saw in the mirror gave me a sick feeling. How could I tell these ladies about the benefits of being a Christian? I froze as I stood in front of the mirror.

I decided to call my friend and tell her I was sick. That was true. I *was* sick. But I couldn't do that, remembering all the cookies she had made and the work she put into this coffee. I would call another friend and ask her to speak in my place. Standing in the bathroom, looking into my miserable face, I realized that I couldn't blame Dawn for my sinful reaction. I had to accept responsibility for my behavior. She was wrong and I was wrong. Two wrongs never make a right.

As my thinking lined up with the truth, I knew what to do about my misery. A familiar Bible verse came to mind: "If we confess our sins, he is faithful and just to forgive us our sins, and to cleanse us from all unrighteousness" I John 1:9 (KJV). I knew my anger was sin and I needed to be cleansed.

Dawn was wrong to disobey me. She was wrong to think that she could slip by me and wear that dress to school. She should have been made to change the dress. The problem was that I was wrong in my attitude as I sought to do the right thing. I was angry: the anger in my heart was confirmed by the words of my mouth and the look on my face! I needed a clean heart and a loving attitude as I attempted to do the right thing toward my little girl.

I bowed my head. My heart was heavy and my eyes were filled with tears. I asked the Lord to forgive me for the anger in my heart. I asked Him to cleanse me and fill me with His love and patience.

My motives were right, but my heart was wrong. It is almost impossible for the human mind to fathom that a heart can be changed. But with one simple prayer, miracles can take place.

I dressed as quickly as possible, and raced to Dawn's school. The principals' secretary paged Dawn on the school intercom, "Dawn Peeples, come to the office."

I saw Dawn coming down the long corridor. When she saw me standing by the desk, her face turned ashen. I know the poor little girl thought her mom was coming to jerk her around just one more time.

Not saying a word, I took her hand and together we walked outside, down the sidewalk, across the grass, and found a place to sit under a tree.

I looked Dawn straight in the eye. "Dawn, I have come to apologize for the way I spoke to you this morning. You were wrong to disobey me. You were wrong to think you could wear your new dress to school when I said you could not. But I was wrong to scream and yell at you the way I did. I have asked the Lord to forgive me for my sin and I must apologize to you. I'm on my way to speak to a group of ladies about being a Christian. God has forgiven me, but I need to make things right between you and me before I can go to this meeting."

Dawn put her head on my shoulder and slipped her arms around my waist. "That's O.K., Mom," she said sympathetically. "We all make mistakes."

Earlier that morning when I had screamed at Dawn, I didn't feel good. I didn't have a physical problem, but I was sick. I was really sick. I couldn't look into my own eyes I felt so badly. My conscience was killing me. I felt guilty. Praise God, my conscience hurt and I suffered from guilt. I suffered from guilt because I *was* guilty! I needed to feel the way I felt. It was not a pleasant feeling, but God's conviction was necessary to motivate me to be obedient to Him, and to make things right with Dawn.

That wasn't the last time God used my little girl to reveal what was in my heart. That wasn't the last time I had to apologize to her either! From that day forward I've been more consistent in accepting responsibility for my behavior. When I'm wrong, I admit it to the Lord and make it right with the other person.

Home Again

Twenty years later Dawn went through a divorce and was left with the responsibility of raising two small boys. We invited her to live with us for a while. When we moved her in, my mind went back to our time together in the school yard under that tree. I know that God had prepared us through that incident for our future.

That day so many years ago marked the beginning of a special closeness between Dawn and me. That was the day I was honest with her, and I feel that was the day her respect for me increased.

When two women live in the same house, use the same kitchen and live with the same two little boys, they better be friends. We both knew that trying to build a friendship after she moved in would be difficult, if not impossible. But through the years we had become friends — and are still friends. Dawn had not changed as a little child. Her mother changed!

Dawn and I made it through one year of living together. We had some days that weren't as good as others! We struggled with wanting our own way. But I knew how to take responsibility for my actions and reactions, to confess my sins and ask the Lord to fill my heart with love. Dawn practiced the same principles. Therefore, we were able to cooperate with each other. We had a wonderful relationship by the time she moved out of our house and into her own apartment.

Because each of us decided to "keep our own hearts," most of the time we made good decisions. We corrected the decisions that weren't good. Making correct decisions produces a clear conscience. When our consciences are not clear, we need to examine the decisions we're making.

Emotions are a vital part of a parent's life. Use them for your benefit. You should have a good feeling about your relationship with your children. Good feelings come when right decisions are made. Right decisions come from acting on the truth. Jesus said, "I am the way, the TRUTH, and the life" John 14:6 (KJV). Truth comes from Him.

Parents have a responsibility to help their children obey the Word of God. We teach them the truth found in the Bible. To be good role models, we must practice what we preach.

What we are to our children is far more important than anything we do for them!

You Can Know

As we said earlier, the first priority of a Christian should be to walk in the Spirit, to let God be in control of your life moment by moment. This is not an option. Paul reminds us of this in Ephesians 5:18, "And be not drunk with wine, wherein is excess; but be filled with the Spirit;" (KJV). Then he describes three ways we can know that God is in control of our life: "speak out to one another in psalms and hymns and spiritual songs. . . making melody with all your heart to the Lord. At all times and for everything giving thanks in the name of our Lord Jesus Christ to God the Father. Be subject to one to another out of reverence for Christ" Ephesians 5:19-21 (AMP).

To give a practical paraphrase:

1. You have a song in your heart and praise on your lips (verse 19).
2. You have a thankful attitude, and willfully give thanks for all things (verse 20).
3. You have a cooperative spirit (verse 21).

This gives you the character to be the person your children need you to be. Wouldn't it be wonderful for your child to have a parent with a happy heart, a thankful attitude and a cooperative spirit? Wouldn't it be wonderful for a parent to have a child with a happy heart, a thankful attitude and a cooperative spirit? Your lifestyle is contagious. Be sure you spread a spirit that is pleasing to the Lord.

Making It Easy

The first commandment in the Bible that contains a promise is made to children. "Children obey your parents in the Lord: for this is right. Honor thy father and mother; which is the first commandment with promise; That it may be well with thee, and thou mayest live long on the earth." Ephesians 6:1-3 (KJV).

Children are to honor their parents. If parents are honorable, it's easy for children to obey this commandment. When parents say their children don't honor them, the question comes to our mind, is the parent honorable?

Honorable parents have their children's respect because their behavior is respectable. You do not command respect. You earn it. Unfortunately, we have had to deal with children who have no respect for their parents. There have been times when we agree with these children. Their parents' behavior is not respectable. But children are commanded to honor their parents whether parents are honorable are not. We have to tell these children they should honor mom and dad because of their position as parents.

Being honorable also makes it easier for parents. Honorable parents can feel good about the job when it is over, and feel good about the job along the way. A clear conscience enables you to have restful nights and peace in your heart through troubled days.

Are You Honorable?

How can you become an honorable parent? The Bible gives us this directive found in Deuteronomy 4:9, "Only take heed to thyself, and keep thy soul diligently, lest thou forget the things which thine eyes have seen, and lest they depart from thy heart all the days of thy life; but teach them to thy sons and thy sons' sons" (KJV).

We are diligent to exercise, diligent to keep abreast of what's happening in the world, diligent to take care of the "things" we possess. Why shouldn't we be diligent to keep our souls?

Notice that this verse instructs us to "take heed to thyself," which means directing your attention away from your children's souls and on to your own soul. Remember our tendency is to allow our child's behavior to determine our emotional condition. This verse begins with the word, "only." Need we say only means ONLY! Your attention should be constantly directed to your soul.

Your soul consists of your mind, your will and your emotion. Begin with the mind. Pay attention to what you store in your mind. Parents need to fill their minds with the Word of God. Herein lies the truth: the truth about God and the truth about human beings. You want to understand your child? Read the Bible.

In this Book you discover what to "be" as well as what to "do". Emotions furnish the "want to". When what we *know* is combined with our *want to*, the will is influenced and a choice is made. Diligent means keep on keeping on. Do not stop!

"Take heed" means to consider and bear in mind. Our translation: "only consider and bear in mind what is coming out of your heart." Keep looking at it, long and hard! There are times when this isn't pleasant. It's difficult to face the truth about yourself when you're angry, impatient and resentful. Harboring anger, impatience and resentment brings on discomfort. It's impossible to accept responsibility for your wrong behavior when you blame your discomfort on your child's misbehavior.

It's disconcerting to hear that you can't blame your child for your discomfort. But if you really want to be free from your discomfort, then truth must be brought to bear. The Bible teaches that you shall know the truth and the truth will make you free. (John 8:32)

You will be easily discouraged if you attempt to change your child in order to remove your discomfort. On the other hand, you will be greatly encouraged when you understand that changing your own heart brings comfort.

Frustration comes when we try to control what we cannot change.
Hope comes when we change what we can control.

Who is Going to Change?

As we've stressed in this chapter, our natural inclination is to pray for our children's behavior to change. There is nothing wrong with praying for your child. God may answer your prayer. However, a change in your child's behavior does not free you from your anger, impatience and resentment. This may be a shocking revelation.

God's purpose for our lives is to conform us to the image of His Son, to cause us to bear His resemblance. The Son of God is loving, gentle, patient, kind, faithful and self-controlled — exactly the character traits a parent needs!

Most parents want to be loving and gentle and kind and patient and have self-control. We want to be faithful to our families. When we are none of the above, we feel that we've failed. These feelings are valid.

The good news is that we don't have to continue to fail. God is faithful to His Word. He said He would change us and change us He will. He has no favorites. His desire is the same for every parent. He waits for us to ask Him to do in us what He promises.

Love comes from the Lord and does not depend on a change in our child's behavior. As we love others, the Bible says, our hearts become holy before God. "And the Lord make you to increase and abound in love one toward another, and toward all men, even as we do toward you: To the end he may stablish your hearts unblamable in holiness before God, even our Father, at the coming of our Lord Jesus Christ with all his saints." I Thessalonians 3:12,13 (KJV).

Follow the Leader

We should be able to recommend our lifestyle to our children and our grandchildren. As Deuteronomy 4:9 says, teach what you've learned to your sons and your son's sons. (Of course this refers to daughters and granddaughters too!) Children will follow someone. Best it be a loving mom, dad, grandmother and grandfather.

What better person to be an example than a parent. It's far better for a child to have a mom or dad as a role model than some stranger down the street. To be a desirable role model involves sacrifice. You may have to sacrifice your anger, bitterness, selfishness and sometimes resentment. You must to be willing to confess these sins and allow the Lord to cleanse you if you want to recommend your lifestyle to your children.

And one day you will have an active role in the lives of your grandchildren as well as your children. What a wonderful thing to be able to confidently recommend the Lord and His ways to them. When you aren't walking with the Lord, it's easy to forget the things the Lord has done. Sam and I feel fortunate that in our bank of memories we have deposited many of the Lord's blessings.This rich deposit allows us to write an abundance of checks for our children and grandchildren. This is only possible because we have tried over the years to be consistent in keeping our souls.

Parents influence their children by their behavior more than by words. Amazing how smart a little child can be. Children see through the actions of parents, but they usually don't understand how to verbalize what they see or they are afraid of the rebuke should they tell the truth about what they see.

All too often, we see children drop their heads, loose the sparkle in their eyes and walk away from a parent who is screaming and "having a fit." It seems the very life goes from the face of the child when a parent goes on a rampage.

When parents go astray, the cost is high for both parents and children, as this poem suggests:

> It was a sheep, not a lamb that strayed
> In the parable Jesus told;
> A grown-up sheep that had gone away
> From the ninety and nine in the fold.
>
> Out in the meadows, out in the cold,
> 'Twas a sheep the Good Shepherd sought;
> Back to the flock, and into the fold,
> 'Twas a sheep the Good Shepherd brought.
>
> And why, for the sheep, should we earnestly long,
> And so earnestly hope and pray?
> Because there is danger, if they go wrong;
> They will lead the young lambs astray.
> For the lambs will follow the sheep, you know,
> Wherever the sheep may stray
> If the sheep go wrong, it will not be long
> 'Til the lambs are as wrong as they.
>
> So with the sheep we earnestly plead,
> For the sake of the lambs today;
> If the lambs are lost, what a terrible cost
> Some sheep may have to pay.

— Author Unknown

Truth That Never Changes

In today's society, we desperately need a set of values to live by. Sam and I were motivated to write this book because we feel those values are found in the Bible. Sad, but true the world in general does not consider a study of the Bible as a vital part of education. It is something people did long ago. If we are to bring back the value the Bible deserves in the lives of people now, it is going to have to be when parents consider it important enough to study.

When you learn parenting principles from the Bible, you are learning truth that never changes. When behavior is based on truth that never changes, behavior never has to change. Habits are being formed. Helping a little child establish good habits and behavior is critical. What is established in the formative years will continue throughout a child's lifetime. Wouldn't it be nice to make sure these habits are formed in relation to the truth!

Parents can "do" and "be" all the right things and children can still turn out wrong. They can make decisions that break your heart. There are times when we can do nothing about our children's decisions.

But when we keep our souls diligently, we will feel good about our job as parents. We took care of our hearts and confessed our sins. If an apology was in order, we apologized. When it ends and it does, we will have the confidence that we followed Biblical principles in performing our responsibilities as parents.

"A happy heart is good medicine and a cheerful mind works healing, but a broken spirit dries the bones"

Proverbs 17:22 (AMP).

Shape Up

Now that we have recommended ways to get in shape for parenting, the following chapters will deal with specific parenting responsibilities. To perform these responsibilities, it is helpful to understand your child. The Bible describes human behavior, including how children behave. Being familiar with this information will enable you to anticipate your child's behavior. In other words, you will know what to expect. Constantly reacting and recovering causes a huge drain on your emotional and physical energy. Anticipating, rather than reacting to problems cuts down dramatically on stress in parenting. This will enable you to conserve energy that you need for the rigorous task of caring for your children.

statement was definitely true. He then told us about his experience raising sheep. Living on a farm outside the city, he had decided to put sheep in his front yard. He made sure the sheep had food and water. But his business kept him too occupied to spend time with the sheep. As he left for his office every day he enjoyed looking at them. One day he returned home to find the sheep dead. What a shock! At the end of the meeting, the man introduced himself to me as Truet Cathy, founder and president of *Chick-fil-A*.

No where is the need for full-time supervision more apparent than in the parenting role. It is critical that parents supervise their children. Parents are also like sheep and need full-time supervision. God has provided a Shepherd for us in the person of Jesus Christ. It is logical that when our children see us following the Good Shepherd, it is easier for them to do the sa ~ Not only will the child have proper leadership, but supervisior ~ security and safety. What a privilege for a child to have ~ is following the Good Shepherd. Sheep follow shee ~ ople!

Why do she ~ n? We'd like to suggest seven reasons. By ι ~ il, you'll readily see how each of these applie ~

Children need full-time sup ~ ise. . .
- they have no sense of direction
- they are untrainable
- they are defenseless
- they fall prey to peer pressure
- they cannot bear heavy burdens
- they need discipline
- they need authority

By comparing the behavior of children to the behavior of sheep, let's look at how this unique approach can offer you new insights into understanding your child.

CHAPTER II

Understanding Your Child

"All we like sheep have gone astray; we have turned every one to his own way; and the Lord hath laid on Him the iniquity of us all."

Isaiah 53:6 (KJV)

Have you ever thought of your child as a sheep? God says we are ALL like sheep! The problem with most of us is we know so little about these animals. Knowing nothing about them makes the analogy meaningless. Out of all animals on earth, God chose to compare human beings to sheep. There must be good reasons.

Many leaders in the Bible began their young lives with shepherding responsibilities. Could it be that God knew learning to care for sheep would be a good school for learning to care for people? Our purpose in introducing this thought is to enable you to be better equipped for the shepherding responsibilities of your children.

Moses was tending the sheep of Jethro, his father-in-law, when God called him to lead the Israelites out of Egypt to the Promised Land. Moses spent the next forty years wandering around the desert leading several million murmuring people. God's preparation for this laborious task was Moses's job of keeping a flock. God never sends His man unprepared. He could have prepared Moses in any number of ways. He chose the school of shepherding. There must be something to be learned about human nature from tending sheep! When God gave him marching orders, Moses switched from sheep to men!

Generations later, the prophet Samuel came to Jesse's home to select a future king for Israel from among his sons. David, the youngest, was not brought in to be interviewed. Certainly Samuel wouldn't be interested in the youngest son who had the insignificant job of caring for sheep. Jesse had the same problem we do today. He didn't understand the value of managing sheep! He didn't seem to realize that this was the means God used to prepare David for leadership. David was told to "shepherd" the people of Israel. His shepherding experience prepared him for leading God's chosen people.

It is our job as parents to provide leadership in the home. Obviously none of us is experienced when our first baby is born. Unfortunately there is no schooling for this responsibility. What can we learn from sheep that will equip us for the task of parenting.

We believe that understanding the analogy of sheep and children offers many valuable insights into understanding children. In fact we've traveled the world studying these interesting animals. In this chapter we'll show you how you can understand your child better by studying the characteristics of how sheep behave.

Full-Time Supervision

First of all, children, like sheep, need full-time supervision. Sheep are the only herd animals that require full-time supervision. When a man decides to raise them, he must commit his life to them. Other herd animals can be fenced, fed, watered and checked on occasionally and they will probably be fine. Not so with sheep! They must be watched during the day and secured at night. In the Middle East, many shepherds bring their sheep into their houses at night.

I was invited to speak at the headquarters of *Chick-fil-A*, a national restaurant chain, in Atlanta, Georgia. While speaking, I made the statement that sheep need full-time supervision. A man in the audience stood up and interrupted me, announcing to everyone that this statement was definitely true. He then told us about his experience raising sheep. Living on a farm outside the city, he had decided to put sheep in his front yard. He made sure the sheep had food and water. But his business kept him too occupied to spend time with the sheep. As he left for his office every day he enjoyed looking at them. One day he returned home to find the sheep dead. What a shock! At the end of the meeting, the man introduced himself to me as Truet Cathy, founder and president of *Chick-fil-A*.

No where is the need for full-time supervision more apparent than in the parenting role. It is critical that parents supervise their children. Parents are also like sheep and need full-time supervision. God has provided a Shepherd for us in the person of Jesus Christ. It is logical that when our children see us following the Good Shepherd, it is easier for them to do the same. Not only will the child have proper leadership, but supervision provides security and safety. What a privilege for a child to have a parent who is following the Good Shepherd. Sheep follow sheep and people follow people!

Why do sheep need full-time supervision? We'd like to suggest seven reasons. By looking at each of these in detail, you'll readily see how each of these applies to your child.

Children need full-time supervision because. . .
- they have no sense of direction
- they are untrainable
- they are defenseless
- they fall prey to peer pressure
- they cannot bear heavy burdens
- they need discipline
- they need authority

By comparing the behavior of children to the behavior of sheep, let's look at how this unique approach can offer you new insights into understanding your child.

No Sense of Direction

Sheep need full-time supervision because they have no sense of direction. Left to themselves, they don't know where to find food or water. They don't know how to avoid danger. All the sheep on earth would soon starve to death or die of thirst, if it were not for the thousands of caring shepherds who constantly oversee their feeding through the seasons, provide water, and control their grazing.

"Nothing is more up-to-date than the vivid imagery in the Parable of the Lost Sheep. Luke 15. Jesus was a master at telling the story and in depicting the psychology of sheep. All other animals would be able to follow the spore, find clues, and track the pack, even hours later-and soon find their way to the herd. But not a sheep! The poor sheep becomes lost, wanders aimlessly, and gives up in panic.

This famed parable graphically illustrates the condition of the sheep-and the sad spiritual state of Mankind alone and without its Shepherd. More than ever before in history, man has become spiritually like a sheep that is lost and is becoming overcome by his growing sense of lostness and all that means.

Modern man, collectively and individually, spiritually needs so desperately The Good Shepherd to find him, to lift him into His caring arms, to place him on His strong shoulders, to love him, feed him, and to be a shepherd to him, bear him home from his terrifying lostness.

In this century, more than ever it seems, the erosion has started in the very foundation of this heritage: the home and family. To mom and dad, to grandma and to granddad before them, the family, the Old Home, the spiritual altar it surrounded, have always been a steady anchor in times of war, sickness, catastrophe, and death.

"Be it ever so humble,
There is no place like home."

Amidst the rapid erosion of human institutions, the home too has come under attack. The statistics are most sobering-and so alarming! The enemy is not just outside the home, but comes from the inner decay of love, values and personal commitment."[1]

Today, as never before, parents need to supervise their children. We cannot leave children to their own way and expect them to follow the paths we desire for them. The Great Shepherd said, "I am the way, the truth and the life..."

Learning NO!

Parents supervise their children by providing instruction that helps them make right choices. Once when our little one-year-old grand-daughter, Lauren, was visiting us, she turned the corner in our home and saw a wonderful set of stairs. A toddler and an inquisitive young lady, she went for the steps. A great new adventure and challenge lay ahead of her.

As her grandmother, I was responsible for supervising her. I told Lauren, no! Lauren looked back at me. It was obvious from the look on her face, she knew the meaning of the word no. She looked at the

---

[1]W. Godfrey Bowen, Why! The Shepherd (San Miguel, CA, 1988), p. 18

steps and back at her grandmother. My expression reinforced what I said. Lauren looked several times at the stairs, then back at me. She turned and walked away to investigate another corner of the house!

If only this happened with every no! Some times physical restraint is called for. We'll talk more about discipline in an upcoming chapter. In this instance, verbal instruction was adequate. It is possible to teach a one-year-old. Lauren could have been seriously injured in climbing those steps. She was ignorant of the danger. I provided the supervision she needed to keep safe. Lauren, like a sheep, was about to turn to her own way. As Lauren's shepherd that day, I helped her to make the right, safe choice.

This may seem insignificant, but it is the accumulation of all these small choices that enable children to walk in the right path. Lauren didn't learn the meaning of no from her grandmother. Her parents taught her this. It's important where you leave your children. A caretaker should support your parental values. It's your responsibility to find out what the caretaker's value system is.

As Lauren's grandmother, I'm developing a relationship with this special little girl. I'm firm and loving when I instruct her. Because we share the same value system with Lauren's parents, she is continuing to respond to authority and therefore feels secure.

Lauren needs supervision. We are not saying she *wants* supervision. A child innately has no clear sense of direction.

Therefore parents must provide guidance and supervision to help children make right choices. If parents are consistent in helping children choose rightly in the formative years, children are likely to continue in this direction when they leave home.

Then you can consider that your parenting responsibilities have been fulfilled. This in no way guarantees that children will go in the right direction. However, it does guarantee that parents can have a clear conscience regarding their parenting duties.

Parents must provide guidance and supervision to help children make right choices.

Untrainable

Trainable animals learn from mistakes. They respond to punishment and remember pain. Sheep don't seem to remember these things. They must constantly be told what to do over and over again. This is why you never see sheep performing on television or in a circus. In Isaiah 53:6, we are told that sheep go astray. This natural tendency further explains why it's impossible to train them. Sam and I saw this demonstrated in the Agrodome in Rotorua, New Zealand.

The Agrodome is a large barn-like structure. Twice each day lectures and demonstrations are given about nineteen different breeds of sheep. As the sheep are introduced, they appear from the rear of the room and walk down each side to a three-level platform to take their places on stage. Each place is labeled with the name of the breed.

I was shocked to see that these sheep had been "trained". My theory about sheep was seriously in question. I whispered to Sam, "Those sheep have been trained!"

Sam whispered back to me, "You cannot train sheep!" He had observed that six of the sheep had failed to go to their proper places. Twice daily for months these sheep were expected to perform in the same way and they still had trouble going where they were supposed to go.

After the performance, we had the privilege of meeting Godfrey Bowen, founder of the Agrodome. I "sheepishly" asked how he had trained those sheep! I trembled as I waited for his answer.

He whipped his head around and said, "You cannot train sheep!"

I breathed a big sigh of relief. Godfrey explained that sheep follow sheep. He had placed pieces of carpet down the aisles of each side of the room. Sheep were paraded back and forth, back and forth until their scent could be picked up. The doors were opened and the sheep would run down the carpet where other sheep had been. This was the only way Godfrey could get the sheep to go to the front of the room where the stage was located.

Two men waited at the stage steps to make sure the sheep went to their proper places. Even with the men there, the sheep tried to turn away and go their own way. The men had to grab them and forcefully direct them up the steps.

This show turned into a comedy for us as we thought about the many times we had stood on the steps and directed our own children to their proper places. In many instances, we had to use force. I remember wondering what was wrong with our children since I had to constantly remind them what they were supposed to do, where they were to go and especially where they were *not* to go! What a relief to realize that like sheep, people need constant supervision.

Training involves repetition. The need for repetition is not necessarily caused by a child's rebellious spirit. The need is there because like sheep we all go astray and want to have our own way. You give guid-

ance for as long as it's necessary. You get what you *inspect*, not what you *expect*! I found that I was wrong to expect my children to remember what I had said after saying it once. The problem was that I didn't want to be interrupted and take the time necessary to shepherd our children. I wanted to say it once and be done with that part of parenting! I felt guilty about this until I realized that I too am like sheep. I want my way and I don't want anyone getting in my way!

Knowledgeable shepherds are aware that sheep are not trainable. Knowledgeable parents are aware that children are not trainable and need full-time supervision.

Defenseless

Sheep also need full-time supervision because they're defenseless. They have no means of defending themselves from outside forces. They don't have sharp teeth to bite predators; they can't run fast; their horns are not sharp enough to ward off enemies.

As parents, we need to be aware that our children are exposed to many immoral influences. Until moral standards are built into children, they can't distinguish right from wrong. The Bible clearly teaches that we are born with a fallen nature. Since Adam fell, human beings have had a bent to do those things that aren't pleasing to God. It's extremely important that we realize children are born with a bent in this direction and do not acquire it with age.

A Biblical value system will enable your child to make the right choices and defend himself from these immoral influences. Our behavior is lived out in front of our children in line with our set of moral values. These may or may not line up with the Bible. As a Christian, it behooves you to constantly monitor your set of moral values to

be sure they are biblical. These values should be practiced both within and without the home. Children are smarter than most of us think. They recognize their parents' inconsistencies.

The greatest need a child has in order to defend himself is to accept Christ as his Savior and to walk in the Spirit. The power of the Holy Spirit will provide the defense needed against the internal influences of the fallen nature and the external influences of secularism. This can be done at an early age. Our daughter, Dawn, became a Christian when she was six years old. She still remembers clearly the day this happened. She was raised in a home that provided a Biblically-oriented value system. However, as a college student she found that many of her professors taught from a secular value system. She was able to discern the difference and her discernment was a strong defense.

Sheep Follow Sheep: Peer Pressure

During a recent visit to Australia we watched sheep moving from one pasture to another. As they walked along the path, they followed in line one after the other. Except for the lead sheep, every sheep was simply following the one in front of him. It didn't seem to matter where they were going. As we stopped our car to watch them, one of the sheep turned his head to look at us. All the other sheep turned their heads and looked at us too. Just like people. To prove the point, go stand on a busy street corner and look up. Need I say what will happen?

It's normal for sheep to follow sheep and it's normal for people to follow people. But you must be careful where your leader is going. Some people are leaders and some are followers. This is what makes society work. Parents have the responsibility to check out who their children are following or where they are leading others.

A shepherd in New Zealand told us that he had accidentally left a sheep in the field when bringing his flock in for the winter. Once the shepherd realized he had lost a sheep, he went back to find it. The shepherd took two sheep with him because a lost sheep won't follow the shepherd, but he will follow other sheep. Without the sheep, the shepherd has to drag or carry the lost sheep home. So he simply took the two sheep and had the lost sheep follow along home.

At an early age, children begin to follow other children. This is normal. A child develops socially as he interacts with other children. The parent's job is to shepherd the child, which means being aware of who your child is following. Parents should be sure that their children are safe with the peer group they have chosen.

In the adolescent years peer pressure based on secular values can be a great enemy. To be in the "in" group, children are challenged to make choices that agree with the values of the group, which are often not the family values they have grown up with.

THE FEAR OF THE SNEER OF THE PEER

When our daughter Dawn went to junior high school, the close mother/daughter relationship we had developed changed suddenly. Dawn would come home from school and retreat to her bedroom. She had nothing to say to me or other family members. She didn't want to spend time with us. Strange behavior for a young girl who had been open and friendly and participated in all family activities up until then.

I was also teaching Bible classes at the time and was a highly visible Christian in the community. Dawn felt ashamed of me. She was afraid her friends in the "in" group would find out about her mom. I tried to talk with her about her attitude, but she refused to talk.

When Dawn was fourteen, she moved with us to Manila, Philippines. She went to school at Faith Academy, a school for children whose parents were missionaries. The teachers were also missionaries. Within two months, Dawn's attitude began to change again. She came back into the family circle. The "in" group at Faith Academy had the same set of moral values that Dawn had. I began to teach Bible classes in Manila and became a visible Christian in that community. The fruitfulness of these classes became known at Faith Academy. They were excited about what the Lord was doing through these classes. People at the school asked Dawn if her mother was teaching these classes. Dawn was now proud to say yes. The "in" group at Faith Academy

approved of Bible classes and lived by a value system based on biblical principles. Dawn's peers held her in high esteem because of her
mother's activities.

Years later Dawn told us what had happened when she attended
these two different schools during her junior high years. The "in"
group at the secular school was rebellious. These young teens rebelled
against any kind of authority, especially parental authority. Dawn seldom rebelled against parental authority. But she found she had to
change to be accepted by the group.

A fourteen-year-old feels a greater need to be accepted by peers than by parents. This is normal for an adolescent. The problem came when the moral values of Dawn's peers were different from her own. The change in Dawn was due to the peer pressure at two very different schools. Dawn had the same family, the same clothes, the same bed — but different friends.

We learned the hard way that Dawn didn't want to defend herself against the peer pressure in the secular school situation. PARENTS: NEVER MINIMIZE THE INFLUENCE OF PEER PRESSURE!

Secular peer pressure can influence children to use drugs and alcohol or become sexually active. This is borne out again and again by statistics. Surveys show that teenage pregnancy is increasing; sexually transmitted diseases are on the rise; experimentation with drugs is occurring at earlier ages and is being abused in greater numbers. Teenage violence is on the increase. Safety in many schools is a major problem.

Children are defenseless in this kind of environment and need full-time supervision. Parents shouldn't be negative in constantly telling children what NOT to do. Instead, be creative in helping them find exciting activities that they'll enjoy.

Children need full-time supervision because they are defenseless against peer pressure.

Not Burden-Bearing

Have you ever seen a sheep pulling a wagon or carrying a load on its back? Have you ever seen a sheep used to plow a field? God says we are like sheep. Since this is true, we aren't able to carry burdens. Hospitals in America are filled with people who have severe health problems due to emotional distress ("burden-bearing" sheep). Parents must learn to cast their burdens on the Lord. Children can be great burdens. "Give your burdens to the Lord. He will carry them. He will not permit the Godly to slip or fall" Psalms 55:22 (TLB).

It was a great relief for us to realize that God loves our children more than we do. He is constantly watching over them. This is impossible for parents. The burden of parenting can be lifted when you begin to trust the Lord to give you wisdom to lead your child. "Let him have *all* your worries and cares, for He is *always* thinking about you and watching *everything* that concerns you" I Peter 5:7 (TLB).

Assuming total responsibility for caring for a child fills parents with fear and anxiety. What a great burden to be responsible for a life. Real-

izing and accepting the truth of the verse above will make that burden light. God is always thinking about you and watching everything that concerns you. This includes your child. If you can't trust God to give you wisdom to care for and lead your child, what can you trust Him for?

As the leader in the home, lead your family as you trust the Lord to lift your burdens. A child learns as he observes!

All too often the burden of making decisions is left with children. Children have little experience or knowledge, and yet parents give them the responsibility to make hard decisions. By not providing guidance, we inadvertently leave them with the task of making decisions for which they are not equipped. How we burden children when they have to make decisions, not having a clue what to do!

Parents are the ones with age and experience. Obviously we should be making the decisions. Of course, as children grow and show responsibility, they should be allowed to make decisions. As we make wise decisions for them, they have this pattern to benefit from as they start to make their own decisions.

Once a friend took her child to a Christian counselor because he was doing poorly in school. This young man was very smart and capable of doing well. The counselor suggested that she let her son fail. What a terrible thing to do! When asked why the counselor wanted to let the boy fail, she was told that he would learn a lesson. We were horrified at this thought and suggested to our friend that her son didn't need to learn from failure. He needed to learn to succeed. The counselor theorized that the boy would be motivated to improve by failing.

We suggested that our friend not allow her bright, capable son to experience failure when it was unnecessary. We recommended that she go home and tell her son that he was not going to fail. He would work and study and succeed. That's what she did. "You are too smart to fail," she told him, "you will study and make good grades."

The boy's parents worked with him and encouraged him to see that this happened. He believed his mom. He worked and ended up with all A's and B's for that year. He's grown now and has a very good job. It certainly wasn't necessary for him to learn by deliberately failing!

Because these conscientious parents were willing to set a goal and supervise their child until the goal was accomplished, this young man avoided the burden of carrying failure. Instead of being ashamed of that year in high school, he's now proud of it.

Subtle Burdens

HAS YOUR CHILD'S BEHAVIOR EVER DETERMINED HOW YOUR DAY GOES?

Remember this question from the first chapter? We asked this question then to make you aware of how parents sometimes look to their children for their own emotional stability. Now we want to change our focus to show what a burden this places on children. Listen to conversations in a grocery store or mall. You'll hear parents say to children, "You're driving me crazy!" or "I can't think because of you!" or "You're making me sick!"

These thoughtless statements put heavy burdens on children. Such statements teach children that their parents' mental and physical health is determined by their behavior. Isn't this too much for a child to bear? Should children learn that other people can determine their mental and physical health? This is a subtle trap we all fall into from time to time. Begin to examine your thinking and conversation to avoid placing this unneeded burden on your child.

Now let's repeat the question with a different emphasis:

HAS *YOUR* BEHAVIOR EVER DETERMINED HOW YOUR CHILD'S DAY GOES?

This subtle trap is one your children can also fall into. Be aware of this possibility and observe your children when your own behavior is wrong. If your children resist your attempts to teach them obedience and their reactions cause them to be unhappy for a few hours or even a day, that can just be part of growing up. However, if your behavior is overly harsh, you could be provoking them to anger. This will place an unnecessary burden on your child. Dealing with resistance in a gentle manner will help your child through the pains of growing up.

Just as your reactions to your children's behavior is the determining factor for your emotional stability, the same can be true for your children. We need to repeat this thought from chapter one:

> *The circumstances of life,*
> *The events of life,*
> *The people around me in life,*
> *Do not make me the way I am,*
> *But reveal the way I am.*

This is just as applicable for your children as it is for you. Your behavior will reveal your child's spirit. This is a difficult truth for parents to grasp. The same is true for your child. The world teaches that we show how much we care by being upset, but this creates a burden for children because they feel responsible.

Your child disobeys, so you punish him. Have you ever spent the entire day with a frown on your face hoping to motivate your child to change? You think that when your child sees how unhappy you are because of his bad behavior he will want to make you happy by changing his behavior. The problem is this doesn't work. The child then feels guilty and burdened. Children often remove themselves from their parents' presence to seek relief. This isn't always possible for small children, but at a later age they can take off! Parents are left to wonder what happened.

The first step in getting help is to identify this truth. Then change the way you think. Realize that your children are responsible for their own reactions. When your children become angry and are uncomfortable, you aren't responsible for their discomfort. Their discomfort is caused by their wrong reactions. Just as you have, your children need to learn to turn to the Lord, confess their sin and ask for a heart of love. We realize that children have to reach a certain age before they can do this. You should be motivated to teach your children this at the earliest possible age since this is a life-changing truth!

Children were not created to bear burdens. And we shouldn't create burdens for them.

Shearing Times

Most sheep are sheared once a year. The longer the wool fiber the more valuable it is. If the fiber is left too long, sheep suffer wool blindness because it turns into the eyeball and destroys the retina. The shepherd needs to know the right time to shear the sheep. Sheep cannot shear themselves or each other; therefore, they must depend upon a shepherd to do the shearing.

The shepherd cares for his sheep and the sheep follow him. Because of this relationship when shearing time comes, sheep trust the shepherd. They're comfortable in the shearing process.

Jesus, the Good Shepherd, knows when we need to be sheared. He takes away something we have been comfortable with. He wants to change us. God's purpose is to conform us to the image of His Son (Romans 8:29). Our greatest fear is the fear of change: our natural tendency is to resist it. This is common for children and adults. The major instrument of change is discipline. Discipline is simply doing what is right when you don't want to, or doing what you ought to do, even when it conflicts with what you want to do. It is our responsibility as parents to discipline our children.

If the parent's value system lines up with the Bible, then discipline helps shape a child's moral character. Lack of discipline is a major problem in America today. We have a generation of young people who were not disciplined. Now they are trying to raise their children. Suddenly they are faced with the awkward task of raising children without any experience in discipline.

Recently, I had a phone call asking me to speak at a women's conference in Dallas, Texas. The lady who called is the mother of preadolescent children. She has founded several Christian schools. She explained her passion for educating and equipping parents with parenting skills based on biblical principles. She was extremely interested in the content of this book and was anxious to receive a copy as soon as possible. Then she explained the reason for her passion. Confirming our own opinion, she said, "We're frustrated because we're a generation of undisciplined people not knowing how to discipline our own children."

Most parents in America feel their chief responsibility in raising children is to keep their children happy. How do you keep children happy? Let them do what they want to when they want to. This sure keeps children from intruding in the plans of parents. Don't forget, parents are like sheep. They want to have their way too! What are we saying? It takes discipline to discipline your children!

Several years ago on a trip to Australia, our host and hostess arranged a visit to a sheep station so we could watch a shepherd shear his sheep. As we entered the large barn-like structure, we saw five sheep in a pen inside the building. The shepherd and his assistant went over to a large bag of feed. They filled both hands with the feed, then they placed their hands through the railing of the pen. Four of the sheep came over immediately and gratefully ate from the shepherd's hands. We noticed that the fifth sheep was running and kicking and playing in the pen. He was ignoring the shepherd. This sheep wasn't interested in taking food from the shepherd.

One of those four sheep was then placed on the stage and the shepherd explained the shearing process as he sheared the sheep. Before we left the building, we asked the shepherd why he fed the sheep before he sheared them. He said he had found that feeding the sheep at that time gave them added confidence and they seemed more comfortable during the shearing process.

Do you know when you're going to be sheared? No one knows when this will happen. There is a valuable lesson to be learned here. We need to be consistently letting the Good Shepherd feed us from His Word. When shearing time comes, we can remember this is in the Shepherd's plan. We can be confident in Him and be comfortable.

We also asked the shepherd why the young, frolicking sheep wasn't interested in the grain it was offered. He said a neighbor had brought this sheep to be sheared. It was a pet and had been spoiled. He didn't attempt to shear spoiled sheep. They resist so much that it's dangerous trying to handle the clippers with their kicking and squirming. Spoiling this sheep made it impossible for the shepherd to shear the sheep. This is also true in the lives of our children. In the Good Shepherd's plan when shearing times come, it will be very difficult because of their kicking and squirming as they resist. Parents should realize how critical it is to discipline their children so that they can conform with the plan of the Good Shepherd.

Isn't it interesting that the owners of the spoiled pet sheep had to turn to a professional to see if he could do the shearing. Does this sound familiar? Who might these professionals be: the police officer, the juvenile authority, a foster parent, the rehab worker?

One Sunday afternoon while writing this chapter, I had a phone call from a dear friend. She told me a story that illustrates well what we are trying to say. Last year Kappy's father, Bill, had by-pass heart surgery. Due to a series of complications, he spent three months in the hospital in and out of the intensive care unit. Several times we heard that he was not expected to live.

Kappy lives in another city and rushed to Birmingham to the hospital on these occasions. These were trying times and a "shearing process" for all the family members. Surprisingly, Kappy told me what a wonderful time these three months had been. You wouldn't expect someone to describe three months of intense concern as wonderful. But she said that the family's strong spiritual foundation became evident as they were drawn together by a serious illness.

For many years this family had been fed by the Good Shepherd and they were comfortable with Him in control of this critical situation. It was hard emotionally and physically, but what a spiritual blessing. Throughout it all, there were more days of laughter than tears.

Kappy had been to our seminar and was familiar with the principles we are describing in this book. We had earlier heard both directly and indirectly that the hospital staff was amazed at how this family handled such a crisis.

Looking back, Kappy is now more confident in the Shepherd. Had she not been in spiritual shape she would have resisted the shearing by the Shepherd.

Clipping for a sheep in shape can be a shear delight!

Shearing is a normal part of life. Your children need to be in shape for it. The way your children handle it will make a big difference in their maturing process.

Wanting Their Own Way

Remember Isaiah 53:6: "All we like sheep have gone astray, each has turned to his own way...." "Wanting their own way" is the only specific characteristic of sheep that Isaiah cites in this verse. The other characteristics of sheep that we've described in this chapter are things that we've discovered from men and women who raise sheep.

Any sheep that goes his own way obviously goes astray and does not follow the shepherd. Sheep may pay a great price for going astray. Straying from the flock with no sense of direction and being defenseless is quite a dilemma.

The nature of human nature is to want to have our own way. People go to any extreme to get their own way. Nowhere is this more clearly illustrated than in watching children. Many times it has been said of an adult, "Wasn't that a childish thing he did?" The next time you hear this, observe closely and you will discover the person being described has done something selfish. It is normal behavior for a child to want to have his own way. Parents should understand this and not react in anger to a young child who keeps pressing to get his way.

My husband loves to tell the following story. It was a momentous occasion when our daughter, Dawn, was old enough to join our first child, Sam Jr., in his playpen. We wanted to record this event. I had the camera in hand ready to take pictures. Little Sam had a playpen crowded with toys. As Sam approached the playpen with Dawn, I was focusing the camera. When our son saw what was about to happen, he began gathering all his toys and placing them in one corner. As Dawn was placed in the playpen, he stood guard in front of his toys. Dawn

saw a particular toy she wanted and began to crawl toward it. When she reached around her brother for the toy, he gave her a karate chop on the arm! Dawn looked at us and began to cry. Her brother began to cry because she was invading his territory. I began to cry because my children couldn't get along! Sam wanted to cry, but being a man he had too much pride. He was trying to decide how this could happen when he realized that this selfish natural tendency had come down through *my* side of the family!

Why did our son act this way? Why did Dawn cry? Why did I cry? Why was Sam perplexed? We each wanted our way and didn't get it. Four different people each wanting their own way. Conclusion: nobody got their way! Sam spanked our son for being selfish. I gave Dawn the toy she wanted to try to console her. Her brother was screaming from the spanking and I got angry at Sam for spanking him so hard. We ended up in a big family argument over how to handle the children. I can't remember how it ended. This was not an event to record with pictures; it was a day we wanted to forget. All this took place because we didn't understand the nature of human nature. We expected entirely too much from our little children. What we wanted them to do was unnatural.

This scene took place before we learned the wisdom of that verse in Isaiah. We thought our children would be happy to share their toys with each other. Keeping this truth in mind can explain a lot of difficulties faced in parenting children.

Parents need to teach their children that they cannot always have their way. Discipline your children and make sure they learn that they cannot have everything they want or have things always go their way. A parent's job is not to keep children happy, but to see that children do what is right.

Our granddaughter, Lauren, has a soft pink blanket that she carries around with her. I took her on a trip to see her great grandmother and the pink blanket went along. It got caught in the car door. I had to take it from her to get it free from the door. She began to cry and hold on to the blanket, which resulted in a tug of war. She was determined not to let me have it and I was determined to take it from her. She didn't know it was dragging outside the car and would be destroyed if I didn't free it. I had to forcefully take this soft pink blanket from my sweet little granddaughter. Her crying was not only a reaction from not getting her way, but a very useful tool to see if her grandmother would change her mind.

We don't consider it abnormal when children cry when they don't get their way. However, when adults cry because they don't get their way, we think this is strange. At what age is it unacceptable to cry when you don't get your way? Twenty? Forty? Sixty?

Lauren cried when she wanted her way. When our daughter Dawn was little, she reacted by pouting when she didn't get her way. She continued to pout in order to get her way. Dawn would go to her room and sit for hours, or even days. She knew if she acted unhappy long enough, I would give in to make her happy. This went on for years. She was a most unhappy child and she had a most unhappy mom. I realized that Dawn was controlling me with her pouting. I was the mom and I was to be in control of my child. I made the decision to let her pout if she chose to do so. If my decision was best for her, I had to stick to it no matter how she reacted.

I told Dawn that pouting was not acceptable behavior. She could choose how she reacted when I didn't let her have her way: she could pout or be happy. The choice was hers, but her choice was not going to alter my decision for what I believed was best for her. Her choice would not determine how my day went!

Years later when Dawn was an adult, she shared with a group of young mothers how she had felt insecure in our relationship because she knew she controlled me. She was confused when I changed, but once she realized that I was not going to give in to her pouting, she felt secure in our relationship.

Dawn has two little boys now. When her first son was about six months old, she told me that she realized each time little Mark cried, she immediately ran to him. Remembering how she had controlled me with her pouting, she realized that Mark was controlling her with his crying. As most moms, Dawn had the ability to discern Mark's cry. She knew a desperate cry from a wail simply to get attention. She needed to be the judge of how fast to run in response to his cry. This was her way of teaching little Mark that she was in control. Being in control provided Mark the authority he needed. A child's reaction — crying, pouting, "pitching a fit" — is the result of something not going his way. If you can learn to think this way, you'll avoid the common questions, "Why is he doing this?" or "What have I done to cause this reaction?"

Children want their own way. Don't let their reactions control you.

The Need for Authority

Children have a built-in need for authority. Of course, they aren't necessarily aware of this. Because they have a natural tendency to resist authority, children show no evidence of this yearning and therefore parents are unaware of their need.

Shepherds who supervise their sheep have satisfied sheep. Through supervision, they provide authority. Without exception, in every sheep-raising country we have visited, shepherds have told us that their presence among the sheep provides a calm sense of security. An authoritative presence provides a positive influence for sheep.

So it is with children. Children need an authoritative figure in the home. In the next chapter we will give you some practical tips for meeting this important need in your child.

CHAPTER 3
PROVIDING
AUTHORITY
AT
HOME

CHAPTER III

Providing Authority At Home

"Children, obey your parents; this is the right thing to do because God has placed them in authority over you."

Ephesians 6:1(TLB)

"Hey, Mom! Hey Dad! Are you ready?" Your child is constantly non-verbally asking that question. You *are* ready when you're spiritually and emotionally prepared, and you understand your child's needs.

Still not sure you're ready? Confidence comes through experience. If you are just starting with your first child or wanting to implement these principles for the first time, we want to encourage you. Your confidence as a parent will only come through day by day experience. Reading books on parenting, this one included, does not take the place of experience. Someone has said that you don't learn to swim by taking a correspondence course. You need to jump in the water. Trust the Lord to build your confidence as you faithfully practice these parenting principles.

In the following chapters we suggest skills you need to succeed in the game of parenting. With the right spirit and consistently practicing these principles, we believe our goal can be accomplished: enabling you to feel good about your parenting job when your responsibility is finished.

We assume you're a parent who walks in the spirit, who desires to have a heart filled with love, joy, peace, patience, and self-control. After reading the last chapter, you understand your children and their needs and you're learning as we did that like sheep gone astray, we all — adults as well as children — turn our own way. Now let's look at how moms and dads, always under the guidance of the Good Shepherd, can provide authority for their flock, giving their children the security and clear direction they so desperately need.

Setting Limits and Boundaries

The day you accepted responsibility for your child you began to set limits. You decided where your baby should sleep. You provided a crib or bed, thus protecting your little one with secure boundaries. The sides of the bed kept the baby safe, and at the same time provided limits. Beyond the edge of that crib your baby could fall to the floor and suffer grave injury.

You can expect children to resist set limits at an early age. Our third child spent many hours in a playpen. He spent his time working at the spokes to loosen them. One day he removed two and crawled out. He took the spokes out and he has been "outspoken" ever since.

This was the same playpen we used for the first two children. With their easy-going temperaments they never tested the limits the way Mark tested them. Little did we know this was his announcement of things to come! Hindsight is always twenty twenty. I am sure Mark thought, with a smile on his face, "I am free, free at last!" He had no way of knowing that his freedom from limits exposed him to many dangers. He could stick a key in the wall sockets; fall down the steps or overturn a table or a chair. New and different limits had to be set.

The need to provide limits is not determined by a child's age. As children grow older, the kind of limits set and the form they take changes. The older children become their resistance to limits becomes more stressful on parents. At these stressful times you will be tempted to reduce or remove the limits. If you do succumb to this temptation, be assured that your child will repeat the same resistance when he tries to remove the limits again. Let's face it, children aren't dumb. Why wouldn't they continue to use something that works? So if you succumb, you can expect more of the same. Please remember this when you face the temptation.

God has given parents the responsibility of providing authority in the home. Providing authority and setting limits gives children a sense of security. What is security? *Webster's Dictionary* defines *security* as "protection; effectual defense or safety from danger of any kind; freedom from fear or apprehension, confidence of safety."

Security is also knowing you're loved. Once we visited a friend who pastored a small church in South Carolina. That evening a group of teenagers held their weekly meeting in his basement. During their rap session, several of them complained about the restrictions their parents had placed on them. One young boy sat quietly in the corner listening. Finally, he spoke up. With tears in his eyes, he said, "I wish my parents cared enough about me to tell me what time to come home. They never ask where I'm going. They don't even know whether I'm home or not."

The other kids turned and looked at him in shock. Here was someone yearning for the very thing they were complaining about. This neglected adolescent expressed the true need of every child. We don't know this boy, but we can guarantee you that he suffered from insecurity due to lack of limits!

Limits provide protection. When clear limits are set, children know if they are inside or outside the boundaries. This gives them freedom from apprehension and confidence when they're within the limits. Established boundaries not only benefit children, but parents as well.

They give parents a clear, fixed reference from which to supervise and when necessary bring correction.

Parents along with their children need to be creative in designing as many enjoyable activities as possible within the boundaries. This helps children have a positive attitude toward boundaries and see them as less threatening.

Flexibility Within the Boundaries

One of the Dallas Cowboys' most famous quarterbacks, Roger Staubach, made an interesting statement in a book about his life. He and his coach, Tom Landry, were reviewing the team's play book soon after the new quarterback joined the team. Staubach was amazed that there were over two hundred different plays in the book.

It takes a lot of creativity to design that many different plays to be executed on such a small piece of ground. If you were to sit in the stands at a football stadium and look down at the field, the boundaries might seem very restrictive. They might even appear to stifle a team's creativity. A football team has two options: take a negative approach and complain to the officials about the boundaries, or take a positive approach and work together to design a variety of plays that can be run within the limits of the field.

Suppose that Tom Landry and his team had decided to spend months pleading with the officials to make the boundaries bigger. Obviously their efforts would've been futile. Fortunately, they didn't do this. Instead, they took the positive approach. Working together, Landry and Staubach launched a team with one of the most successful records in the NFL.

With a positive attitude, it's amazing what you can do within boundaries and enjoy the game. This is true with parenting too. You can expect your children to take the negative approach, and on many occasions relentlessly plead with you to broaden the limits you have set. Hopefully, this football illustration will remind you of the importance of sticking to established boundaries.

If your children openly resist your rules — getting angry or upset — let them "cool off," then sit down with them and work together to design a variety of pleasurable activities they can enjoy within the limits.

As we've said, children by nature resist, question and at times reject authority. How they do this varies according to each child's personality and temperament.

Our first son was very compliant and appeared to be cooperative. He was so quiet and reserved that he went about getting his way and doing what he wanted to in a manner that went unnoticed. Our second child was also compliant and cooperative. So we assumed all children were this way.

What a shock to have number three and discover how different he was! Mark wasn't rebellious. It was simply the contrast that was so confusing and frustrating. Sam Jr. was quietly resistant; Dawn pouted when she resisted and Mark was outspoken as he resisted. Just as the squeaky wheel gets the grease, so Mark got most of our attention. It was years later before we realized that our older son was equally as resistant as our younger son. Their personalities were so different we were deceived into believing we only had one highly resistant son. We fell into a trap by comparing our sons one with the other.

Reading Isaiah 53:6 and realizing it teaches that "all" want their way and "all" go astray, I began to think about our children. Was our compliant son Sam included in "all"? Of course he was! It wasn't until Sam was married and was a father himself that this thought occurred to me.

One day I called him on the phone and asked him if he had been a "sneak". He laughed and said, "Mom, what's happened to you?"

I laughed too and said, "I just realized that everyone wants their own way and that must include you! You always seemed to do what I said with no resistance. Now I wonder if you secretly resisted by being quiet and doing what you wanted to do. In other words, did you sneak around unnoticed in such a way that you never got caught?"

There was a pause in our conversation. I could hear him chuckle. "Sure, I did!"

We trust you will re-evaluate your children and not fall into the trap we feel into.

When our friend, Dr. Henry Brandt, was visiting us on one occasion, we asked him about some family matters. He asked us a series of questions regarding Mark, our strong-willed son. Can you depend on him to challenge your authority? We answered, yes. Is he consistent in doing this? We answered, yes. Is he very tenacious in trying to get his way? Again we answered, yes. He then said, "You have a dependable, consistent, tenacious son."

He asked, "Do you have any problem with those qualities?" The obvious answer was no. He advised us to be patient and consistent in our efforts, keep him in the boundaries and direct him in the right path. "Can you imagine what would happen if these qualities were focused in the right direction?" he challenged us. "Don't try to change these qualities. Be patient and help him direct these qualities toward positive goals."

When Mark focused these character traits on positive goals, Dr. Brandt said, there was no telling what he could accomplish. We weren't impressed with Dr. Brandt's counsel. We felt he didn't understand our son and our circumstances. However, we're happy to report that after many years had gone by, this wise family counselor proved to be correct.

We knew that we had a strong-willed child and assumed this was a problem. Most parents consider strong-willed children problem children because it takes more time to discipline them. They require more supervision and they can easily become an interruption in your life.

However, raising strong-willed children can be viewed in a positive light. They can be equally determined to do what is right when they have positive attitudes and goals. Parents need to provide an example and atmosphere conducive for such a child to make right choices.

Today our strong-willed son is married and they have a little girl. With a new set of responsibilities and his character traits focused on being a good husband, father and employee, he is a successful young man.

Attitude vs. Behavior

A parent's role is to help a child learn to respect and submit to authority. This authority is exercised in the area of your children's behavior. There are no guarantees that your efforts will produce the right attitude. But what a relief to realize we aren't responsible for our children's attitude! God deals with the heart. He is the only One who can change a person's heart. How confused and frustrated parents and children become when parents attempt to force a change in their children's attitude.

We put the cart before the horse when we work on our children's attitude believing this will have a positive effect on their behavior.

It's true that in the Christian life our behavior should be motivated by the right attitude. But the Lord is the One who develops an attitude which is pleasing to Him. A child must be willing to let the Lord do this. Until this occurs in a child's heart, parents should provide authority and supervise their children's behavior.

For many years I lectured and punished our children for having a bad attitude. During these years I felt like a failure as a mom. I felt like a failure because I was failing! I could successfully make our children act as if they had a good attitude, but there is a big difference between *acting* polite and happy and *being* polite and happy.

Again Dr. Brandt advised me to change my focus from their attitude to their behavior. At first, I resisted this approach. But this man was wise and had years of experience. I decided to try what he suggested. Instead of trying to force an attitude change, I began to concentrate my efforts on helping my children do what I told them to do.

One day I asked Mark to cut the grass in the front yard. As was his habit, he started complaining. "Why do I have to cut the grass? I always have to cut the grass. I hate cutting the grass."

I listened and asked God to put love in my heart for this boy who was giving me such a hard time. I never said a word about his complaints. Finally, I looked him in the eye and said, "You can cut the grass mad or glad. That's your choice. You just have to cut the grass."

He looked startled, but he went out and cut the grass. It was an unusually hot day. When he finished the job, I met him at the front door with a tall glass of cold ice tea. He was hot and dirty, but he was proud of his work. "Mom, the yard looks good, doesn't it!"

I smiled. "Mark, you did a great job. Thanks."

That was the end of the confrontation. He did what I asked him to do. The grass got cut. Because he obeyed, he felt good about himself. This experience was part of the process in his gradual change of attitude.

There is a proverb that sheds immense light on this subject. "Commit thy works unto the Lord, and thy thoughts will be established" Proverbs 16:3 (KJV).

To make this verse more applicable to this principle, we can substitute the word "behavior" for "works" and the word "attitude" for "thoughts." Try reading the verse this way: "Commit your behavior to the Lord and your attitude shall be established." Until children commit their behavior to the Lord, parents need to influence their behavior by seeing that they do what is expected of them.

An incident between our two grandsons further illustrates this point. Both boys are the same age. When they were five years old, little Sam hit Mark. As far as anyone knew, there was no reason for this fight. Sam just decided to hit his cousin. He dealt a mighty blow and Mark fell to the floor. Mark began to scream and cry.

Sam's father ran to see what had happened. He comforted his nephew and then asked his son to apologize. Little Sam said, "no."

His dad looked hard at him and said, "You tell Mark that you are sorry you hit him."

Sam looked back at his dad and said, "no!"

His dad said, "You tell Mark you are sorry you hit him or I will take you into the bathroom and give you a spanking." Again, Sam looked at his dad and said, "no."

Off to the bathroom went father and son. I heard the spanking and the screams. When they came out, my son said to his little boy, "Now, tell Mark you are sorry you hit him."

Sam said, "no." My son announced that if he did not obey, he would receive another spanking.

Up until this time, I had been a good mother and kept my mouth shut. I was preparing dinner and gritting my teeth. But I couldn't stand it any longer.

I asked my son to step outside with me. I had to laugh because little Sam was not going to tell a lie. He hit Mark because he wanted to. He probably would have enjoyed hitting him again. He wasn't sorry and he wasn't going to say he was sorry.

I asked Sam to please stop trying to make little Sam say he was sorry for something he had apparently enjoyed doing and for which he was not sorry. My son said, "What am I suppose to do? Let him go around beating up other children?"

Sam should have been punished for his behavior. My son was sorry Sam hit Mark and was embarrassed about his son's behavior. I suggested that he punish Sam and tell Mark that he was sorry for what had happened.

Our son was trying to force an attitude change. He was not able to do this. He was trying to force Sam to say he was sorry when he really wasn't sorry. If Sam wasn't sorry and was forced to say he was, he was being taught to be deceitful. The spanking was for wrong behavior. Obviously it had no effect on Sam's attitude.

As we've stressed in this chapter, one of the key responsibilities of parents is to help children learn to respect and submit to authority.

While in New Zealand, I thought of this incident as we watched a sheep dog work to bring some sheep into a pen. The sheep had been in the pasture and the dog was sent to round them up, bring them to the barn and guide them into a pen. The dog brought the sheep to the barn, but was having a difficult time getting them into the pen. The sheep got to the door of the pen and stopped. The dog stared at the sheep. The sheep stared at the dog. The dog crouched and slowly edged nearer the sheep. The dog fixed his eyes on the sheep. A man standing next to me whispered to his wife, "We have a Mexican stand off!"

We waited and watched to see who would win. Suddenly one of the sheep staring at the dog, raised his right front leg and stomped it to the ground. The other sheep followed suit. The sheep continued to stare at the dog and stomp their right front feet. What a picture of human nature. Those sheep without a word were saying to the dog, "I will not go in the pen and you can't make me!" We laughed realizing that on many occasions, this was a perfect picture of our children and grandchildren.

When we accept Christ as our Savior and Lord, we submit ourselves to His authority. By training our children to submit to authority, the decision to place themselves under Christ's authority should be easier. Some day when our children consider whether to accept Christ as Lord of their lives, hopefully this will not be a stumbling block. This in itself should be enough motivation for Christian parents to provide consistent authority.

Don't Fence Me In!

As you drive through the country and pass through cattle farming areas, it's humorous sometimes to see cows with their heads and necks protruding through strands of barbed wire, trying to get to the grass on the other side. The cows seem to think the grass on the other side of the fence must taste better. Often the barbed wire is bowed out from the pressure and a barb has cut into a cow's neck causing bleeding. Is the effort and pain worth it just to reach this forbidden and seemingly "tastier" grass! Often the grass the cows are standing in appears to be exactly the same as the grass on the other side of the fence.

And yet, even as adult Christians, don't we find ourselves straining against God's law and His boundaries, not aware of all the provisions we have in Christ *within* the boundaries?

There was a time in Alabama when some counties didn't have fence laws for cattle. I remember crossing a county line and suddenly there were no fences. Beside the road, I saw a dead cow, apparently struck by a car. What a contrast: one cow straining against the fence (providing security) and another cow dead beside the road. I have often wondered if the dead cow had second thoughts about the fence after being struck by the car!

The same is true of the boundaries on a football field as we said earlier. These boundaries don't restrict the game — they are an absolute necessity. They provide a framework in which all the players feel secure in executing their assignments. Can you imagine playing without them?

As a farmer provides for his cows and officials provide for players, so parents should provide boundaries for their children. Both mom and dad need to agree on the boundaries. Parents should have a strong commitment to be like-minded regarding boundaries. This prevents children from playing mom against dad. Children quickly learn who to go to and for what! When they do this, there is often a breakdown between mom and dad.

A lack of commitment to make and honor these agreements means the family suffers. First, mom and dad are angry at each other. The parent who did not honor the agreement rushes to the child and reverses the decision. The child becomes angry with the parent and resists the change in decision. The parent becomes angry at the child's resistance. Does this scene sound familiar? You can prevent this painful experience by following the principles laid out here. An ounce of prevention is worth ten pounds of cure!

First, both parents need to agree on who will announce the rules or boundaries to the children. Usually one parent is better than the other in communicating with the children. It doesn't matter who makes the announcement. What does matter is that the best communicator makes it.

You can expect resistance. This resistance represents the child's efforts to get his own way. By now you've learned to understand the nature of your child, and this shouldn't surprise you. At this point you will need to examine your reactions to this resistance.

Dealing With Anger

Janie attended a Parenting seminar I taught. She wanted an appointment to talk to me because she didn't believe what I said applied to her situation. She told me the following story:

"It was Christmas and the T.V. "soaps" were alive with the season as beautiful women shimmered in gowns of red and green; toasted with champagne by dashing and handsome young men. I looked away from the T.V. and gazed out our kitchen window. In comparison to the soaps, my life seemed to be missing something. As I finished washing dishes, I could see the rose garden fading with the coming chill of winter. Christmas is my favorite season, yet that day my heart was full of sadness. I felt my life was fading just like the rose garden.

I had every reason to be happy. I had a hard working, handsome husband. I had two healthy children and I lived in a large house with a housekeeper and a gardener.

The problem was that I was sick of being a mom and I wanted out. My little boy was waking at 4:30 a.m. and staying awake for the day. I am not a morning person. On this day I cried out to God and prayed, "This is your last chance with me, and I am sick of this mess." I told Him, "If I am wrong in the way I do things you show me." Suddenly I felt afraid and at the same time a sense of relief.

I waited and watched for an answer to that prayer but nothing happened right away. I had expected an immediate answer.

In January, my sister invited me to your seminar. I went to get away from the kids. To my surprise, everything you said to do, I was not doing with my children. I knew either you were wrong or I was wrong. I decided you were wrong and I was right! "

Janie brought four pages of notes. Most of the information described her screaming quick tempered son. When Janie finished reviewing her notes I said, "Janie, you have a very smart, hot tempered little boy. When he's older you can teach him to confess his sin so he won't blow up." Janie seemed stunned! She realized that she blew up at him when he blew up at her. She confess to me that she had been angry with this little boy since the day he was born.

God answered Janie's prayer that day. She didn't want me to know how shocked she was to hear the truth. She left my office with tears streaming down her face. Later she told me that she confessed her sin of anger for the first time as she drove home. She said, "I asked God's forgiveness for the anger I had held onto and the bitterness I had toward that little boy. I asked God to fill my heart with love and patience for him. Beginning that day, my life changed because I now had hope for a better relationship with my son."

Janie said, "I realized my screaming at him and spanking him in anger had to stop. A new way of parenting was before me." She told me about their conversation the next day. She said that was their first real conversation. She invited him to come sit with her and talk. He replied, "You want to talk to me?" He moved forward a few steps. She urged him to sit with her. He looked at Janie as if she would bite! She said, "This was the first time I treated him as a person and he didn't know what to make of this "new" mom."

This little boy barely sat on the edge of the wicker sofa as if preparing to make a get-away. Janie said her voice cracked as she said, "Jimmy, Mamma has made a big mistake." He replied, "You have? What did you do?" She said, "I scream at you and spank you when I am mad." Jimmy said, "You sure do that alot to me." Janie asked Jimmy to forgive her. She told him she was sorry for the way she had treated him. He jumped up, threw his arms around her and said, "Oh, I love you Mamma and I always forgive you." This was the first time Jimmy had ever told Janie that he loved her. Janie said, "What a reward for letting go of anger and bitterness."

Janie said that she had learned a wonderful truth, "Happiness is found in a heart that is right with God. I was looking around me for happiness before. Today, my life is not without problems, but I pay close attention to how I react to those problems."

Janie realized that Jimmy had crossed her from the day he was born. She told me, "I thank God for his life and how He used him to reach me. The calmer I faced his temper tantrums, the less I saw them. I discovered I had more energy, because I was not staying mad all the time. I can say today that I no longer feel trapped, for it was truly the only Son of God, our Lord Jesus Christ, who touched my heart and changed my life." It is common for parents to react in anger to a child's resistance. This angry reaction is damaging whether it is expressed to the child or held inside. If you don't deal with your anger, your attempts to carry out your responsibilities as the authority figure will be motivated by anger.

How do you deal with your anger? Do you repress it? Express or vent it? Perhaps you're tried biofeedback or medication. "Expressing" and "repressing" are human terms and are not found in the Bible. Both are equally wrong. The Bible teaches that the correct way to deal with anger is to confess it. "If we confess our sins," Scripture says, "he is faithful and just to forgive us our sins, and to cleanse us from all unrighteousness" I John 1:9 (KJV).

Here God tells us to confess "sin"! Obviously, you must first regard anger as sin. Many Christians are reluctant to do this because they don't want to give up their angry reaction even though they agree it isn't good for them.

For several years this seemed strange to us. As we listened to people's stories, we realized that anger is a good weapon many of us use to get our own way. Isn't it amazing that we are more concerned with having our way than dealing with damaging anger.

If you doubt that anger is damaging, several years ago a well-known physician wrote a best seller entitled, *Your Anger Can Kill You*. In it he quoted from a number of case studies documenting his claim. It's amazing to us, as counselors, that the medical profession is more concerned about the physical damage of anger than Christians are about its spiritual and emotional damage! I can guarantee you that none of those death certificates from the documented cases listed the cause of death as unresolved anger. Yet the physician clearly showed that anger was the primary cause of the negative physical changes which eventually were fatal. Two well known Christian psychiatrists have said that the chief cause of death is unresolved anger.

For those of us who want to get our way most of the time, we'd be foolish to give up our best tool. The following story illustrates someone who didn't deal with anger well.

Bob and Sue were on extension phones describing the sudden change in their son's behavior. Both voices were crying out in desperation. I had to ask them to speak one at the time. They were calling to make an appointment for me to see their son, an appointment they wanted as soon as possible. Like today!

I told them about our policy. We first talk to parents before meeting with children. So we made an appointment with Bob and Sue. During our session, Bob and Sue spoke in generalities about their cooperative thirteen-year-old son who now at fourteen had become rebellious. Their chief complaint was his acute temper tantrums. I was puzzled, and yet curious. I had heard of temper tantrums, but not "acute" temper tantrums. Finally, I asked for a specific example.

Bob recounted a recent incident. Jim's class at school had planned a bowling party. Bob and Sue decided Jim shouldn't go to the party because it was on a school night and Jim would be out too late. When Sue told her son about their decision, Jim had an acute temper tantrum.

Sue was shocked and not sure how to handle this new situation. That evening she told Bob what had happened. Bob confronted Jim about his unacceptable behavior. Bob suddenly witnessed another tantrum. Everything seemed to be settled until breakfast the next morning.

Jim announced that he was going to the bowling party. Bob said this had been settled and there was no need for further discussion. You guessed it — Jim responded with another tantrum!

Jim's mother, Sue, and his little sister, Betty, left the table. It was simply too uncomfortable for them to stay there. Bob settled back in the chair in my office, threw up his hands and said, "This is what we have to put up with!" I was interested in Bob's reaction to his son's acute temper tantrums. I asked Bob to tell me how he reacted. After a long pause, while he began loosening his collar, he awkwardly admitted that he DID have a "short fuse"! He was very angry and he had lashed out at Jim. I was curious to know what he meant by a short fuse. What would a man look like with a short fuse?

Picture the scene. We have a child who uses an "acute temper tantrum" to get his way. We have a father who uses a "short fuse" to get his way. We have a mother who tries to get her way by leaving the scene. Neither Bob nor Sue's efforts seemed to have any influence on Jim's tantrums.

I explained to Bob that Jim had learned to use anger as an effective means of getting his way. Why wouldn't Jim use something that works? Jim had a great teacher in his own home. Suddenly Bob's face went pale. Isn't it amazing that an acute temper tantrum is unacceptable, but a short fuse is acceptable?

More recently a couple came seeking counsel for their strong-willed rebellious son. Their story was almost identical to Bob and Sue's. The only exception was that instead of having a "short fuse," the father said he goes "ballistic."

I spent the rest of my appointment with Bob and Sue showing Bob how to deal with his anger and still be a strong authority figure in the home. Most parents aren't sure this is possible. It is much more effective for a kind, gentle, pleasant father to deal with his angry, screaming son. Once you confess your anger, which means agreeing with God that it *is* sin, He forgives and cleanses you of that sin. When God removes the anger through cleansing, you should ask Him to replace it with love.

God can cause your love to "increase and abound" even toward a rebellious son (see I Thessalonians 3:12). Children have a tendency to

be influenced by a loving father much more than by a father with a short fuse or one who goes ballistic. This rule goes for moms as well. Who do you allow to influence you? Those who love you and are gentle with their persuasion, or those who lash out and attack you?

Like sheep we need a shepherd. We need a shepherd to lead us in the right direction as we give direction to our children. Remember, only God can change a heart. This can only happen when we are willing to turn to the Lord, repent and seek help in changing. We can act as if we aren't angry, but only God can take the anger out and replace it with love.

Bob realized he needed to work on himself. He couldn't change the hearts of Jim, Sue or Betty, but he could allow the Lord to change his heart. He asked the Lord to do that for him.

Bob and Sue never requested an appointment for Jim. Several weeks later I talked with Sue. She was excited as she described the change in their home. I asked her if Jim had changed that much? She smiled and calmly said, "No, but his mom and dad are changing and it's making a difference not only in our lives, but in the atmosphere of our home."

It's remarkable what can happen from one counseling session when parents are willing to practice the truth. These parents have eight to ten years left to raise Jim. Our goal in counseling parents is to equip them to patiently and consistently perform their biblical roles as parents.

A Soft Answer

- *"A soft answer turns away wrath; but grievous words stir up anger"*
  Proverbs 15:1 (AMP).
- *"By long forbearing and calmness of spirit a judge or ruler is persuaded, and soft speech breaks down the most bonelike resistance"*
  Proverbs 25:15 (AMP).
- *"The beginning of strife is as when water first trickles (from a crack in a dam): therefore, stop contention before it becomes worse and quarreling breaks out"*
  Proverbs 17:14 (AMP).

When our strong-willed son was a senior in high school, he was voted the most outstanding defensive player on the football team. He was a linebacker — six feet tall, two hundred and ten pounds of muscle and a seventeen-inch neck. He was popular with both boys and girls. Our house was always filled with his friends. Girls loved to bring his favorite pie and cookies to the house. Each year the senior class at Mark's high school went to Florida for spring break. In February, Mark approached me about going on the senior trip. I said he could go if either his dad or I went with him.

His favorite expression that year was, "Excuse me?" He fired this at me. I repeated my answer, "You can go, and your dad or I will go with you." Mark was horrified! Linebacker, most valuable player, seventeen-inch neck and his mother was going with him to Florida for the senior trip!

He screamed, "I am sick of you. I am sick of the rules in this house. I am sick of Christianity and people around here saying, 'Praise the Lord'. I'm leaving this place. I'm running away. You're making a fool of me and I hate you for that."

Mark followed me around the house continuing to let me know that he was not going to take this treatment any longer. The more he talked, the angrier I became. I was ready to explode. My only escape was the bathroom. I excused myself and locked the bathroom door.

He would not invade my privacy. Mark stood outside, beating his fist on the door and exclaiming, "Do you hear me, mother? I'm leaving."

I bowed my head and prayed: "Lord, outside this door is a two hundred and ten-pound linebacker. I'm his mother and he hates me. Lord, I'm so sick of him. I'm sick of his mouth. I'm sick of his screaming at me. I will be so glad to get him out of here. Lord, at this moment Mark needs a mom who loves him. He's an angry, hostile young man and he doesn't need an angry, hostile mom. Please forgive me for my sin. Forgive me for the anger and resentment and bitterness I feel toward my son. Forgive me for wanting him to leave. Oh Lord, please take away my sin and replace it with love, patience and acceptance for Mark."

I came out of the bathroom. Mark continued to follow me around the house for a few minutes. When he got no response from me, he went to his room. The house was silent.

I went into the kitchen to prepare dinner. After a while, Mark appeared and asked if he could take out the garbage. "Thanks, it doesn't need taking out," I said.

"Do you need me to go to the store for you?" he asked.

"No, thanks, I have everything I need."

Mark was apologizing. This was his way of saying I'm sorry. That wasn't the way I wanted him to apologize. I wanted him to crawl on his knees and say, "Precious mother, I'm sorry for the way I talked to you. Please forgive me." Until this day he has still not said he was sorry, but I know he was.

I had to make a very important decision. Could I accept Mark's apology his way or did it have to be done my way? I decided to accept it his way. As far as I was concerned, his offer to help was an apology and the issue was settled.

Sam went to Florida with Mark. He took some paper work and spent time in his room, and Mark never complained about his dad being there.

While our children were growing up, we never allowed them to drink or smoke. We made that decision because of their health. Drinking and smoking are deadly habits. We assume that Mark was glad to be able to tell the guys and girls that his dad was around and he would suffer serious consequences if he was caught drinking. His dad's presence was a boundary for Mark. This boundary was erected to protect him, not serve as punishment. We love Mark and wanted him safe as he enjoyed his time in Florida.

During Mark's outbursts, I had turned to the Lord and asked Him to change my heart. This did not guarantee a change in Mark's heart. Many years went by before we began to see a change in him. Sam and I had to take our own advice. We could wait for Mark to change either mad or glad. We decided it would be best for all of us if we waited glad!

When Mark was twenty-nine, he married a lovely young lady named Nancy. They had a beautiful church wedding with all the frills. As Sam and I came out of the church, we saw Mark and Nancy standing beside a big, black limousine that was to take them to the reception. The driver, in uniform and cap, stood by the back door waiting to open it for them. What were they waiting for? They should have been in the car and on their way.

As we stepped down the steps of the church, Mark dropped Nancy's hand and stepped forward. Six feet tall and now weighing about two hundred and thirty, he was easily able to lift me off my feet. He didn't say anything. He just picked me up and held me tightly in his arms.

After a few seconds, he lowered me to the sidewalk, turned to Nancy and took her hand. The newlyweds got into the limo and took off for the reception. I stood on the sidewalk in front of the church and watched the long, black car drive away. I could see Mark and Nancy's heads through the rear window. After two blocks, the car turned left and disappeared.

I prayed, "Thank you, Lord, for the bathroom. Thank you for hearing my prayers and changing my heart. You took out the anger and resentment and replaced it with love. Thank you that because of the change you made in me, I was not constantly provoking Mark. It was never a barrier in the way of improving our relationship.

What a great reward for such a sacrifice. It's a sacrifice to give up your anger when your child is attacking you. You want to lash back. "I'm not going to take that from him," you seethe. Your natural instinct prods you to fight back. But fighting back always destroys peace. Mark was an angry son who needed to live in a peaceful home with a loving mom. Maintaining a peaceful home with a loving mom didn't mean that the boundaries were altered or removed. They remained intact.

Mark and Nancy now have a beautiful little girl. We see them responding to her in a loving way. Maybe Mark learned this from growing up in a home where his parents' goal was to be loving.

The love of parents for their children should never depend on the children's behavior. When this is the case, the child controls the parent. This breeds insecurity in a child.

When children resist authority, parents should decide how long to interact with them. Reasoning seldom changes a child's mind. Children need to know rules are debatable, but not negotiable. If boundaries are to be re-set, parents should negotiate changes.

Once the boundaries are set and family rules established, it's time to enter the game of parenting.

A Game Plan

Before the game begins, mom and dad put on their black and white striped shirts and become referees. As referees, parents need to agree on what type of "penalties" are needed and how severe they should be. It is very important that the referees cooperate. Any changes in the family rule book need to be a joint effort and not a solo decision! This confuses children and also creates problems between the referees.

In the "family game" parents are not only the referees, but also the coaches. The coaches develop a game plan and are responsible for its execution. In the heat of the game, it often appears as if the game plan isn't working. At this point it's easy for the players (children) to become frustrated and discouraged. In looking from the field to the sidelines, the last thing children need to see is the coaches arguing!

If it appears that you're loosing the game, don't change or abandon the game plan. Rules don't have to be set in concrete. However, any alterations or changes should be made by the parents. Mom and dad should have the freedom to explain why changes need to be made, and children should also have an opportunity to express their opinions. But changes should never be made based solely on the opinions and/or resistance from a child or children.

It is a parent's responsibility to train children, but responsibility without authority causes frustration. That's why there are so many frustrated parents today. They're frustrated because they're attempt to carry out their responsibility without being willing to exercise authority. Society tells us that being too authoritative might emotionally damage a child. But isn't it emotionally disturbing for a child to live with an angry, hostile, bitter parent? Authority provides security. Anger and bitterness result in insecurity.

Commitment and Involvement

Now comes the tough and time consuming part of the game plan. Once the rules and boundaries have been established, parents have to enforce them. This takes careful supervision. There's an old management principle that is very applicable to raising children: "You get what you *inspect*, not what you *expect*." Remember this as you formulate your family game plan. As you consider each part of the plan, ask the question, "Are we willing to supervise this, (inspect)? If not, then it shouldn't be a part of the plan. When children see that you don't back up what you say by supervision, your words have no value. They wonder, how can we know what mom or dad really mean when they tell us what to do? That's a legitimate question.

Children are born wanting to get their way and they can be very ingenious in their efforts to get it. Sam can remember coming home one evening and driving up the driveway. Before he could get out of his car, one of the children was there with a question. "Daddy, can I ride my bike over to John's house?" Of course, Sam had not checked with me yet. When he told the children he would have to check with me, he watched their faces turn to disappointment. He knew what had happened. They had already asked me and I said no.

Cooperation and harmony are necessary ground rules in designing a family game plan. If one parent gives in under pressure or is soft on certain issues, the child knows who to ask. I have seen children play their parents one against the other like experienced professionals.

Whenever a request comes that hasn't been previously agreed upon, then always check with your husband or wife.

Parents also need to agree on who will supervise each part of the plan. Supervision needs to be a joint effort, requiring personal commitment and involvement.

In December of Mark's senior year in high school, I got a call from the principal asking if I was aware that Mark wasn't going to graduate in June. I was so shocked I could hardly catch my breath. This was the year that Sam and I had launched our family counseling ministry. My first thought was, "What will my friends think of me!" My second thought was to kill Mark! I knew that wasn't feasible, so I quickly moved to my third thought: "I'll keep this quiet, send him on a Caribbean cruise and tell my friends the boat left the day before graduation. When he returns, he can go to summer school, graduate and leave for college with his friends. My reputation will be safe and Mark will be out of here!"

All these thoughts ran through my mind before I ever called to break the news to Sam. Suddenly as if someone had hit me in the chest with a baseball, I had a terrible pain. I realized just how selfish I really was. Here my son was in trouble and needed help. Who did I think of first? Not Mark, but me! Mark cares about what others think of him too. How he must have suffered alone because of his impending failure.

I dropped on my knees and cried as I asked the Lord to forgive me for being so selfish. I asked Him to give us wisdom to help Mark through this hard time. I called Sam and asked him to come home. He called the school and made an appointment with the teacher and principal.

Meeting with Mark's government teacher and the principal, we learned that Mark had failed to even begin a two-semester project.

This project required work each week putting together a large scrapbook. Students had to write to candidates running for office; these letters and their replies were to be placed in the scrapbook. The scrapbook also had to include regional newspaper articles and many other items and documents. Mark's teacher showed us his scrapbook. Mark was months behind, and had failed the first semester.

The teacher was gracious, but said she didn't believe he could finish the work since he was so far behind. She asked if we had received the notices describing the deficiencies? Of course we hadn't seen them because Mark had never given them to us.

Once we calmed down, we discussed what should be done. We got all the requirements from the teacher and devised a plan. We divided the work by the days remaining. If Mark kept to the plan, he could complete his work in time for graduation. The teacher and the principal assured us that if he completed this project with a 'B' grade and passed his other exams, he would graduate.

Mark was eighteen. We knew that punishments never worked for him: we could spank him, put him in his room or deny him something and it never had any effect. We agreed that the goal was to see Mark complete the work and graduate on time. The past was history. No need for trauma. Sam decided to spend the needed time to inspect Mark's work. He was the best inspector; I was the best announcer.

Mark wasn't aware that the principal had called us, and he didn't know we had visited his school. When he came home from school, I met him at the front door with a big smile. "Mark, I have good news for you!" I said. "You can graduate from high school in May!"

Words are inadequate to describe the look on Mark's face. "Mom, what are you talking about?"

"Mark, Dad and I spent a long time with your government teacher and the principal today. They assured us that you can graduate if you complete the scrapbook and pass all your exams."

Mark said, "Mom, there is no way I can do that. I am too far behind."

"Dad has worked it all out for you," I said. "He went to the office and when he comes home, he will explain it to you."

With that announcement, we went to the kitchen for our usual afternoon snack. Mark was in shock. He couldn't believe that we weren't going to punish, attack or hound him about what he'd done.

At dinner that evening Sam explained the plan and the rules. Mark was told that he would finish this project and graduate with his class. No other option was available.

Every Friday afternoon Sam would carefully check the week's work. If Mark was behind, he couldn't leave the house until it was completed. The first couple of weeks things went well. Then late one Friday afternoon Sam asked to see the scrapbook. Mark assured him it was up to date and not to worry about it. After several more excuses, Sam examined the scrapbook and found Mark was several days behind. After dinner Mark and Sam sat down to work. Mark pleaded with Sam to let him go to the basketball game; he promised to work on the scrapbook the next day. Sam said no. Sam and I canceled our plans for the evening. Sam sat down with Mark until 1:30 in the morning until he completed the week's work. Sam didn't do any of the work for Mark. He read, as he inspected!

This seemed to get Mark's attention and we didn't have to repeat that episode. We had set a completion date two weeks before school ended as a buffer if Mark needed it. He finished on schedule and turned the scrapbook into his teacher two weeks early. In December Mark's work had been turned in grossly incomplete and late. With our intense involvement and encouragement, the scrapbook now looked neat and thorough. Mark was proud of his work. The teacher was shocked when she saw it. We teased Mark, suggesting that he take an ammonia capsule for his teacher when he turned it in.

Mark passed the final exam and received an 'A' on the scrapbook. This allowed him to pass the course and he graduated with his class. When he brought home the report sheet from the scrapbook, it was graded in twelve different categories. Each mark was an 'A' or 'B'. Mark was beaming as he showed it to us. We were all excited! Sam tacked the grade sheet on the wall just inside the door to Mark's bedroom. It served as a great reminder of what commitment and discipline could accomplish. The grade sheet stayed there for many months.

On graduation day, Mark had a positive self-image. He had done what was expected of him and he felt good about himself! What a sharp contrast to his attitude and countenance in December when his failure to follow instructions meant he wasn't going to graduate.

One of our favorite Proverbs describes the problem: "He that refuseth instruction despiseth his own soul..." Proverbs 15:32 (KJV). Another favorite Proverb provides the solution: "He that getteth wisdom loveth his own soul..." Proverbs 19:8(KJV).

A Good Self-Image

Providing authority, setting limits and careful supervision play a strong part in helping a child develop a good self-image. It also helps you, the parent, to feel good about your job when your responsibility is ended. If a good self-image is one of your goals for your child, we encourage you to put into practice the principles in this chapter.

As we said, some counselors suggest that you let your child learn through failure. This is an option. Sam and I choose not to go this route. We wanted Mark to learn from success. It would've been easier for us to sit back and let him fail. We didn't consider this an option.

Options are available in every situation. Be careful how you exercise them. Keep reading to understand the role of options in raising children.

CHAPTER IV

The Use of Options

"Say just a simple "Yes, I will or No, I won't". Your word is enough. To strengthen your promise with a vow shows that something is wrong."

Matthew 5:37(TLB)

Options: What Not to Do

Susan tried to remember what her mother had told her when she left for the party: "You must be home at 11:00 or you can't see or talk to Jim for one week." It was now 10:40 and the band was playing until 11:30. Susan's mother didn't know that Jim was leaving the next day with his family for a two-week vacation. Susan decided to stay at the party. She was having a great time and she didn't want to go home until it ended.

Susan and Jim left at 11:40 and took their time getting home. Ellen, Susan's mother, was at the door waiting when Susan walked in the door. It was 11:55. "Where have you been?" Ellen said. "I've been frantic. I told you to be home at 11:00. I'm sick of your indifference to our rules, your being disrespectful to me and your terrible attitude! Go to your room!"

Susan went to her room and began to undress for bed. Ellen went to her room and just as she pulled down the covers, she remembered one more thing she needed to say to Susan. She jerked open Susan's door, stuck her head inside the room and shouted, "Don't forget you are not to see or speak with Jim for one week!" She slammed the door and went into her bedroom.

Susan climbed into bed and pulled the covers up to her chin. "I'll be glad to get out of this house," she thought. "I'm sick of my mother. I'm tired of her insults. I'll never treat my children this way!"

Ellen climbed into bed, thinking, "I'm sick of Susan's attitude. This is the thanks I get for all I've done for her. She never appreciates any-

thing I do. She never wants to spend time with me!" Angry and disappointed, both mother and daughter drifted off to sleep.

What Went Wrong?!

Let's analyze what happened. Ellen gave Susan an option. She told her to be home at 11:00 or she couldn't see Jim for a week. The rule had been established: Susan was supposed to be home at 11:00. If she didn't obey, she couldn't see or talk with Jim for one week. The punishment became an option.

Susan knew she was supposed to be home at 11:00, and she exercised her option. Whether Jim was going to be on vacation or not, the fun of that party was more important than not being able to see or talk to Jim.

Ellen was angry because of the option Susan choose, and yet she allowed it. Susan knew what the rule was, but felt it was O.K. to break it if she was willing to take the punishment. In this case she had information her mother didn't have; therefore, the punishment didn't pose a threat. Let's suppose Jim was going to be home. Do you think she would've stayed at the party? Children tend to be preoccupied with the excitement of the moment. Like Scarlet O'Hara in the movie, Gone With The Wind, they'll think about the punishment tomorrow!

What Am I Trying To Do?

When parents give direction, their goal is obedience. However, options can counteract obedience. Parents all too often back themselves into a corner by using options as a threat. The effective use of options is giving your child a choice that you can live with. Using punishment as one of the choices is a misuse of options because parents find themselves forced to punish while their real goal, obedience, hasn't been accomplished at all. In most homes, although the goal is obedience, far too much punishment is meted out.

Susan didn't disobey her mother. Her mother offered her daughter an option as a means of motivating Susan to be home at 11:00. She wasn't aware that she was giving Susan a choice, but on this occasion Ellen provided Susan with an exception to the rule she had established. In Susan's mind taking the punishment overruled the 11:00 curfew.

Ellen should have told Susan to be home at 11:00. Period. There should have been no "or's," "if's," or "but's". If Susan came in late, she would've been punished for disobeying. It would've been clear in both Ellen and Susan's minds that Susan had disobeyed the rule. Choosing a wrong option would never have entered the picture.

Ellen reacted in anger to Susan's decision to come in at 11:55, which is a dangerous trap for parents to fall into. The Bible warns, "Fathers, do not irritate and provoke your children to anger - do not exasperate them to resentment - but rear them (tenderly) in the training and discipline and the counsel and admonition of the Lord" Ephesians 6:4 (AMP).

We can include mothers as well as fathers in this verse. Parents should discipline their children, but not provoke them to anger. For this reason the first chapter in this book was devoted to the spiritual well-being of parents. If Ellen had met Susan at the door and calmly announced the punishment, Susan probably would've been angry, but her anger wouldn't have been provoked by her mother. Ellen was using her anger to impress upon Susan how serious her disobedience was.

We've had many parents ask us, "If you don't get angry, how is your child going to know that you mean what you are saying?" We gently point out that if their angry instructions had produced a change in their child's behavior, they wouldn't be calling us for help. Don't look for new ways to keep doing the wrong thing! Don't continue to perpetuate failure! The Bible recommends a better way to train your child:

"But, speaking the truth in love, may to grow up into him in all things who is the head, even Christ"

Ephesians 4:15 (KJV).

You may very well be speaking the truth. We realize that. But are you speaking the truth in love? Love is long-suffering and kind. Love bears all things, endures all things and at the same time love never fails (I Corinthians 13:4-8a). Let's face it — raising children *is* long-suffering! You'll have to endure many loooooong days, yet wouldn't it be wonderful to have something inside you that God says will never fail. In all our years of searching the Scriptures, we've never found a verse that promises that anger never fails. God's way is best!

For most parents this is a difficult habit to break. But if you examine your spirit before you talk with your child, and correct it if necessary, you can form a righteous habit. That means you'll begin doing things the right way.

Habits are First Cobwebs, Then Cables

You may have a cumbersome, many-stranded cable woven together from years of perpetuating this bad habit. As you seek to change, your first efforts may seem difficult. Most cables are broken one strand at a time. But remember that as you continue, you will be weaving a new strong cable that will sustain you. The Lord was not involved as you wove the wrong cable, but He will be with you in weaving the right one. Be patient because it won't take as long to build the right one as it did the wrong one. God is faithful.

If Ellen had confessed her anger and asked the Lord to give her a loving, calm spirit, she could have gone to bed without any anger or hostility, knowing that she hadn't provoked her child to anger. A calm announcement is no guarantee that your child won't respond in anger. But your conscience will be clear because you have spoken the truth in love.

There is a subtle advantage in not announcing the punishment beforehand. Children are left to wonder, "What will happen if I don't obey?" In most cases the imagined punishment is worse than anything the parent has in mind. Can't you see them running through scene after scene as they contemplate disobeying. "My mom will kill me if I don't get home!" "There's no telling what my dad is gonna do if I am not home on time!" "I'm in big trouble if I am late getting home!" Let the suspense work to your advantage! Also, let the suspense work to your children's advantage because it is healthy for them to obey!

If obedience is the goal, how can it be accomplished in the situation we described? How can Ellen get Susan home? Our answer may seem radical to you, yet it's very simple. You should know where your children go. If they're not home when the time comes for them to be home, we suggest that you go and get them. We wish we could see your face when you read this! Remember, as a loving, kind, parent you're going to bring your child home. If you choose to do this, she will be embarrassed and possibly angry when you show up at the party to take her home. You probably won't have to do this too many times!

Get A Head Start!

Avoiding embarrassment is a much stronger motivation than punishment. If you aren't sure, give it a try! As we've said before, obedience is the goal. And training helps children obey.

Training should begin at an early age. Statistical evidence shows that children's habits and patterns of behavior are formed in the first five years of life. This type of training requires more time than most parents are willing to give, but it's well worth it.

We watched our one-year-old granddaughter crawl to the steps in our house. She put both hands on the first step and was thinking about how to get the right knee up on that step. These were steep steps leading to the second floor of the house. Since Lauren was a climber, her parents worried that she might hurt herself on the steps in their house. As grandparents we want to cooperate with the parents. I told Nancy, Lauren's mother, if she didn't want Lauren to climb steps, she shouldn't allow her to do it!

"But how do I stop her?" asked Nancy.

I suggested that she simply tell her no, then move her away from the steps. No options, no threats, just a no and a move!

"But she will keep going back," said Nancy.

I laughed. "That's my granddaughter — determined!" I told Nancy to move her away each time she approached the steps. It's best to distract a child at this point. Never put her down near the steps and expect her to stay away, I suggested. Give her a toy to play with or get her interested in something else in another area of the house. At some point if she continues to attempt to climb the steps, give her a pop on the leg. No options, no threats, just instruction and help!

Remembering what I told Nancy, I wanted to do the same. It was time for me to practice what I preached! I said, "No, Lauren, you cannot go up the steps."

Lauren froze. She stared straight ahead and refused to look at me. Her leg was in the air, ready for the climb. I picked her up and took her outside to look at the flowers.

I'm sure this won't be the last time she tests me, but I believe if I'm consistent, she will soon learn the boundaries in our house. She'll enjoy playing within the boundaries, and we'll enjoy having her visit us. We feel that establishing her patterns of obedience is important enough to take the required time. If you're interested in giving your child a positive self-image, start working with them at an early age.

If we allow Lauren to refuse instruction, the Bible says, she won't like herself. "He that refuseth instruction despiseth his own soul..." Proverbs 15:32 (KJV). On the other hand, if she learns to obey, she will be developing a healthy self-image.

The Halls Are Alive With The Sound of Music

David was a very bright young boy. His parents had spent many hours reading to him and stimulating his interest in a wide variety of subjects. I spent time with him when he was only three years old and I was amazed at his capacity to learn and his eagerness to sit and listen to a story. I read a *National Geographic* magazine to this three-year-old and he loved it!

By the time David was in the fourth grade, he was considered a gifted student. He had been double promoted and was in all the accelerated classes. One day his mother, Martha, called to ask if we had any books on how to discipline a gifted child.

She began to cry as she told me what had happened to David. Because he always finished his work before the other students, Martha said David had a problem with boredom. He had to sit idly and wait for the class to finish.

One morning David finished his math and began to sing aloud in class. His teacher looked up and told David to stop singing. David kept singing. The teacher asked him the second time to stop singing. David kept singing. The teacher stood and said in a loud voice, "David, stop singing, or you can go stand in the hall!" David got up from his desk and walked to the hall as he continued to sing.

In a few minutes David's teacher stormed out into the hall and took him to the principal. She demanded that he be suspended from school for three days for his insolent attitude. She told the principal that David had insulted her by leaving the classroom. Martha was called to come to the school to take David home. Let's review this case. We have two people who acted incorrectly, David and his teacher. David disobeyed the teacher's instructions to stop singing, but when she gave him the options to stop singing or go stand in the hall, he exercised his option. Once the option was given, it offered an exception to the rule. The teacher made the same mistake Ellen had made. The punishment became an option. She should have made David stop singing in the classroom. The breakdown came when the teacher got angry. David provoked his teacher to anger, and then she lost control.

David's teacher gave him the option of standing in the hall as a means of motivating him to stop singing. She never dreamed he would take her at her word! She was caught off guard when he left the classroom. Now she didn't know what to do. David was insolent and the teacher was angry. She was determined to win, so the punishment had to be increased. The increase in punishment was no longer for singing, but for choosing the wrong option. David was suspended for taking his teacher at her own word! All the principles in the earlier story about Ellen and her daughter also apply to Martha and her son.

Martha needed to understand what the teacher had done. I wondered if she was doing this in her own home. She didn't need to repeat the same mistake the teacher made. Then I helped her see that she simply had a disobedient child who happened to be gifted. You discipline a gifted child in the same way you discipline an average student. The Bible doesn't have a special set of instructions or principles for gifted children.

Martha just couldn't understand David's behavior at school; he was always obedient at home. I asked if she had told David to mind his teacher. She answered, "Of course I have!"

"Did you tell him this when he was at home?" I asked.

There was silence on the telephone. Martha groaned. She said, "What am I going to do?" I told her the answer is simple, make David do what he is told. It may not be simple to find ways to do this, but the principle isn't complicated.

In the following chapter we'll deal specifically with disciple vs. punishment. A punishment often comes in the form of an option. We have purposefully given you examples of children of different ages to illustrate that the wrong use of options applies to children in all age groups.

A Basket Case

In the grocery store, I often hear a mother say to a toddler standing in the grocery cart, "Sit down or I'll spank you!" Usually I stop my shopping to see what happens next. Most toddlers will take a spanking any day rather than sit down in the cart. I have to chuckle as I watch mom back herself into a corner. Now she must ignore what she said or create a scene by spanking her child. If the mother wants the child to sit down, she should say, "Sit down." Period. Then she should help the child sit down without a reprimand or a scene, which would allow her to peacefully continue her shopping. She may have to repeat this several times. But which is preferable: a scene with an angry

mother spanking a screaming child, or a calm mother offering no option and helping her child obey?

When you take your child to the grocery store, take something to use as a distraction if it becomes necessary. Tell the child to sit down and give him a toy to play with or a cookie to munch on. Get his mind on what's in his hand and off standing in the cart. This will usually help you avoid the embarrassment of having a screaming child in the grocery store.

Not training a child to obey slowly results in the child controlling the parent. Our daughter-in-law realized that if she couldn't control Lauren, she couldn't take her out with her friends. She suddenly realized that Lauren was controlling her because she was limited in what she could do and where she could go. The same is true of the mother in the grocery store. Soon she wouldn't be able to go to the store without arranging for someone to care for her child. Eventually her child would even control when she shopped.

If you get control over your children when they're one-year- old, it will be much easier than waiting until they are teen-age!

Using Options Effectively

Options are valid when either choice is acceptable. Be sure that on the other side of "or" there isn't the threat of punishment. Would you like chocolate or vanilla ice cream? Do you want to wear your blue dress or your yellow dress? You may go skating or to Joe's house to watch a movie. The car is available on Friday or Saturday night. We need to know by tomorrow night which is acceptable to you.

It is a good thing to give your children freedom of choice. Giving children choices helps in their maturing process. When they make decisions on their own, children feel you have confidence in them. But always be sure the options you offer are acceptable choices.

If you aren't offering your children any options at all, you may be too controlling. Self-examination might be very beneficial.

Opposites Attract?

The importance of decision-making really hit home recently as we counseled a couple in their twenties. The young wife said that her husband had grown up in a home with a very controlling mother. He was accustomed to others making decisions for him. Therefore, he had very little confidence in making many of his own decisions. As he dated, he was attracted to a girl who was comfortable in helping people make decisions. The wife admitted that she was a controlling person. This match-up worked well in the first three years of marriage. Now she complained that many of his requests for direction were becoming petty and far too numerous. The fact that her husband wasn't comfortable making decisions for his family annoyed her. What initially had been an attraction now became a burden.

Counseling this couple, we found ourselves trying to train a twenty-nine-year-old how to begin to make decisions on his own. The wife's annoyance was due to the growing number of negative reactions she had because of her husband's inability to make decisions. In order to help her, we suggested she learn to stop controlling her husband and take care of herself. (Refer to chapter one again to remind yourself of how to deal with reactions.) They both agreed that balance was the goal, not simply that she should stop making any decisions and he start making them all. This story points out the need to train your children in the decision-making process.

As we said earlier, we've noticed that the last generation has been raised with a lack of discipline. They never had it, so they aren't aware that children need it. And sadly, once they become aware of the need for discipline they don't know how to provide it.

There is a lot of confusion about the difference between discipline and punishment. Discipline and punishment are not the same. They don't accomplish the same goals. Do you know the difference? Would you like to know? If so, the next chapter will be of great value to you.

CHAPTER 5

HEIR CONDITIONING —
THE IMPORTANCE
OF DISCIPLINE

CHAPTER V

Heir Conditioning —
The Importance of Discipline

"Discipline your son and he will give you happiness and peace of mind."
Proverbs 29:17 (TLB)

Bill, a retired professional football player, had played as a lineman for ten years with a major NFL team. He was a BIG man! But he was intimidated by a tiny little girl — his daughter.

In great distress, Bill called for some advice about how to handle his nine-year-old. Amy, he said, was out of control. Whenever she didn't get her way, she had severe temper tantrums and tore up the house. Because he couldn't control her, Bill resorted to locking her in the bathroom. Confined to the bathroom, she broke the mirror, pulled the towel rod off the wall and stopped up the toilet with toilet paper.

"I don't know what to do with Amy," Bill moaned. "I'm sick of repair bills. I'm desperate. Please help me!"

I sat quietly looking at this man. I could hardly believe what he was saying. I was curious to know how much Amy weighed. He told me she only weighed about sixty-five pounds.

I wanted to laugh. Here was a giant of a man, a very accomplished athlete, who couldn't control a tiny nine-year-old. I asked him what he did when Amy had one of her tantrums. He couldn't do a thing, he said, because he was afraid of injuring her. I could understand his concern as I looked at the muscles in his arms.

But if Bill and his wife couldn't get Amy under control, they would have to call in outside help. We talked about how Bill and Sara handled Amy's misbehavior. Their typical pattern was to allow Amy to misbehave until she became destructive. Bill's anger would build up inside of him until he exploded with a verbal outburst. When Bill yelled, Amy panicked and fought back. She became violent and Bill got scared. Full of anger and aware of his size and strength, Bill was afraid to touch her. So she wrecked the house.

This was a serious situation. Amy needed to be disciplined and her parents needed to do the job. Bill had two major problems. First, he allowed Amy's bad behavior to go on too long and second, the longer she misbehaved, the angrier he became.

I suggested that as soon as Amy misbehaved, Bill should get up and go stop her, rather than sitting and watching until he was frustrated, angry and fed-up! If he waited and allowed her to continue, he then had to take care of his own anger before he could turn his attention to Amy. I made sure Bill knew how to confess and let go of his anger. (This was covered in chapter one. Remember?)

Bill and Amy both needed discipline. Discipline is doing what is right when you don't want to. Bill needed to break an old habit. Instead of waiting, he needed to get up out of his chair and go to Amy. Wanting to be left alone to read the evening paper or watch his favorite TV show, Bill viewed Amy as an interruption in his life. Amy was doing something she wasn't suppose to do and she was happy doing it. She didn't want to be stopped.

Before Bill got out of his chair, I suggested he should calmly ask Amy to stop. If she didn't, he needed to get up and go help her stop instead of staying seated and yelling louder and louder. I had already asked if his yelling had been effective. He answered, no! Why perpetuate failure? Here was an example of someone trying to find help to do the wrong thing in a new and better way.

Because of Amy's age and her instant violence it was useless to try to distract her. Bill needed to calmly go to Amy and restrain her until she settled down. If Bill told Amy to do something, then he needed to help her accomplish the task. By "helping" we are not suggesting that Bill do it for her, but that he gently, but firmly make sure that she followed through on what he had asked her to do. If she needed to stop doing something, he needed to remove her from the scene.

Don't lose sight of the fact that children want their way. Amy had found that by provoking her parents, which brought them discomfort, they let would her do whatever she wanted to do or not do. Peace at any price!

I told Bill that he would have to be patient and consistent with this plan. One or two times probably would not produce results. But, I encouraged him, that doing this consistently eventually would bring about a change in Amy. And I could assure Bill that he would feel better about himself immediately because in taking this approach, he would be dealing with Amy before he got angry. If he did get angry, he needed to quickly confess it to the Lord and ask for love, patience and a calm attitude.

I didn't hear from Bill again for several months. Perhaps he didn't like my advice, I thought. Then one day I saw him in the grocery store. I didn't know whether to say something or slip down another aisle to avoid embarrassing him. He spotted me and threw up his hand to wave. He suddenly broke into a big smile and said, "Mrs. Peeples, come meet Amy." He apologized for not calling to let me know how things were going. Then he made my day! Actually, he made my year! He told me that he had followed my advice to the letter, and he couldn't believe what had happened to him and was gradually happening to Amy.

There stood Amy. A beautiful young lady with a big smile. Bill had told her about coming to see me and she said, "Mrs. Peeples, I'm so glad to meet you." I couldn't believe how poised she was. I knew why Amy was glad to meet me. She didn't have to say anything more! Her nonverbal communication to me was loud and clear. I was delighted.

Many of today's undisciplined young parents are in a dilemma as they struggle to solve their children's problems. Because they weren't disciplined growing up, they don't recognize that discipline is the solution to many of these problems.

What is Discipline?

All too often discipline and punishment are used interchangeably. In Noah Webster's first dictionary (published in 1828) *discipline* is defined this way: "To instruct or educate; to prepare by instructing in correct principles and habits." Discipline comes from the Latin word *disco* which means "to learn". The word *disciple* comes from the same root word. Webster defines a disciple as, "A learner; one who receives or professes to receive instruction from another; a follower; an adherent to the doctrines of another. Hence the constant attendants of Christ were called his disciples; and hence all Christians are called his disciples, as they profess to learn and receive his doctrines and precepts." Isn't it refreshing to see these thoughts in a Webster's dictionary!

In order to make this practical, we define discipline as, "Doing what is right when you don't want to." This is what I told Bill, the frustrated father who didn't want to get up out of his chair and correct his daughter. When you want to do what is right, no discipline is required. Here's another way of defining discipline: "When you do what you ought to do even though what you want to do conflicts with what you ought to do!" It takes no discipline when what you want to do lines up with what you ought to do! The difficulty comes when you realize you have to make a choice. If we do "what comes naturally," we'll always choose to do what we want to do.

We believe parents are the best people to teach and prepare children for a lifetime of instruction and discipline. In the following letter, taken from Dr. Henry Brandt's book, *I Want To Enjoy My Children*,[1] a father writes his son as he graduates from college:

Dear Son,

I'm sure you are thrilled by the idea of taking your place at last in adult affairs - a station of life you probably look upon as a time when "big people" will stop telling you to do things...or not to do things. Your dad has found out that the chains of adult life are wrought of stiffer stuff than the feeble fetters of childhood.

Believe me, no one ever suffered a furrowed brow from such simple commands as "Eat your cereal"..."Do your homework"..."Report for band practice." What once may have seemed a terribly harsh order, "Put away your

---

[1]Henry Brandt, I Want To Enjoy My Children, (Grand Rapids, Michigan: Zondervan Publishing House, 1975) p. 156-157

comic book," will pale into insignificance when compared with an order from the doctor: "Cut out all pastries and sweets."

The bigger you get the bigger other people seem to get - if not bigger in stature, then bigger in authority. For example, did you see the look on Dad's face when the Internal Revenue man ordered him to report to the collector's office with last year's tax receipts? When a traffic officer says, "Pull over to the curb," Dad pulls. When grandmother says, "Roll up the window," Dad rolls up.

I just want to prepare you for a lifetime of saying, "Yes, sir," to master sergeants, shop foremen, loan company executives, bank tellers, tradesmen, public officials, car dealers, game wardens, and a host of other people you never dreamed were your superiors. Even the most politely phrased commands like "Please remit," or "Kindly step back in the bus," are still commands.

Ushers will order you down an aisle; headwaiters will tell you where to sit; courts will summon you for jury duty; the city hall will notify you to shovel the snow off your sidewalk.

You will be dragged off to parties at other people's houses and dragged out of bed by people who come to your house. You will be kept off the grass by policemen and kept up by weekend guests. You will be put on committees and put off buses. This is the true life beyond commencement. Congratulations and good luck.

Dad

P.S. Get a haircut.

As this wise father points out, we have to live under authority throughout all stages of our lives. There are countless times when we are confronted with things we don't want to do. We must make choices. Forming a habit of choosing to do what one should do is very beneficial. As children grow older, the consequences for disobedience can be quite harsh. Parents can begin helping their children form these habits at an early age — the earlier the better.

Helping Your Child Obey

Don't loose sight of the goal. Obedience is what we're after! When we say "obedience," we mean helping children do what you tell them to do. Give serious thought to what you tell children to do. Ask yourself two questions: first, is there a way to help them obey and second, am I willing to be that involved in their lives? Your answers to these questions will reflect how important you consider discipline and obedience. If you weigh what you tell your children to do with these questions in mind, you'll make fewer demands. It's better to ask them to do a few things with discipline and obedience, than a lot of things without them. To help your child obey, follow these three principles:

1. Tell your child one time what you want her to do.
2. Get out of your chair and go to your child.
3. Take the child by the hand and help her do what you told her to do.

We can just imagine what you're thinking after reading the these suggestions! You may be thinking what we first thought when we heard this, "Are you kidding!?" Get up and take them by the hand? This sounds like "doing" for the child. Later we understood that helping means making sure that obedience is accomplished.

Meemaw On The Run

I remember a vivid example of this. One Christmas our four-year-old grandson, Gil, came to visit. There was a candy jar sitting on the coffee table in our living room. (Christmas is the only time I put candy out for the children). Dawn, Gil's mom, had asked me not to let him have any candy before dinner. Gil went for the candy jar as any normal four-year-old would. "Meemaw I want some candy," he begged.

I shook my head. "Gil, you cannot have any candy until after dinner."

Gil looked at me, put his hand in the jar and took a big handful of candy! "Gil, put the candy back in the jar," I said firmly.

Gil looked me in the eye and threw the candy on the floor. When I went to help him put the candy in the jar, he ran through the house, out the back door and down a hill toward the creek! I ran after him. As soon as Gil saw his Meemaw running after him, he started to scream. You'd think I was going to torture him! Believe it or not, I caught him. I picked him up, screaming and kicking, put him on my hip and took him back into the house. I never said one word on the trip back. I put Gil on the floor and with his hand in mine, we picked up the candy and put it in the candy jar. I was exhausted and Gil was shocked. I sat back in my chair and he climbed up in my lap, and put his head on my chest. We sat quietly for a few minutes, then Gil jumped out of my lap and went off to play.

This is what we mean by helping! I have had to help Gil several times since then, but we've never had another traumatic incident like that. Gil is nine years old now and visits us several times a week. We enjoy having him because he has learned to obey us. He knows that when we tell him to do something we intend for him to do it and we'll get out of our chair to see that he does it. Children aren't excited about parents or grandparents helping them. They want to do things themselves. But Gil, along with our other two grandsons, knows our rules. We love having all of them visit because they're disciplined and give us great enjoyment.

If they didn't mind us, we would dread their visits. We would be miserable with them in our home and they would wonder why their grandparents didn't want them around!

A New Way of Thinking

Most parents try to get children to obey the way Sam and I did before we learned and benefited from this principle. We would sit in a chair and tell our children over and over again what to do. With each "over" our voices got louder and louder. Finally, when we reached the loudest level, we got up and punished them for not obeying! During one of Dr. Brandt's visits, he asked me a strange question: "Why have you trained your children to obey when you raise your voice?"

"I don't know any other way," I said. Then he told us about the method we're sharing with you.

As soon as we put this into practice, it changed the entire atmosphere of our house. We want to emphasize this point for two reasons. First, you and your children will benefit, and you'll both have a sense of well-being because you're doing what's right. Secondly, when your children grow up and become parents, they will do it "like we did it at our house!"

"And now a word to you parents. Don't keep on scolding and nagging your children, making them angry and resentful rather, bring them up with the loving discipline the Lord himself approves, with suggestions and godly advice" Ephesians 6:4 (TLB).

By telling children what to do over and over, you're nagging. We began to realize that loving discipline, and nagging and scolding didn't go together. What "the Lord approves" is clearly stated in this verse.

One afternoon, Sam went to pick up our grandsons, Gil and Mark, after school. He was late getting there and searched the school grounds for the boys. Finally, he found them. Gil saw his granddad and ran to the car. Mark saw his granddad and kept playing. Sam called out to Mark, "Come on, let's go!" Mark continued to play. Sam called over and over again and Mark continued to play.

Sam decided to walk to the car, certain that Mark would stop playing and follow him. If he saw his granddad walking to the car and realized he was going to be left behind, surely he would come to the car. Wrong! Mark continued to play. Sam was getting angry. He got in the car, drove away and left Mark on the school playground. That would show him! Surely Mark would panic and run after the car. This would teach him to disobey his grandfather. As Sam drove away, he looked in the rear view mirror and saw Mark continuing to play. Sam laughed. Suddenly, he realized what he was doing. He was handling the situation in the wrong way. Recalling the principle we've talking about, he stopped, backed up, parked the car, got out, walked all the way across the playground, took Mark by the hand and walked him to the car.

Obviously, knowing this principle doesn't mean you'll practice it every time. But hopefully, you'll remember and correct yourself if you're wrong. You notice that Sam didn't punish Mark. It was Sam who made the mistake. He should have called once and then gone to bring Mark to the car. Sam helped him obey so punishment wasn't necessary. Is the goal obedience or punishment? Once we started using this approach, we found that obedience was occurring more and more and punishment was needed less and less.

This may be a new way of thinking for you. That's one reason we are writing this book. In working with parents we have found that

they immediately see their situation as an exception. Please, give it a try before you settle for the exception. If your way of getting your children to obey isn't working, don't look for new ways to keep doing it wrong!

Consequences and Punishment

Punishment is discomfort inflicted on a child as a result of disobedience. Discomfort teaches a child that disobedience has a consequence, and facing consequences is a vital part of training children.

"Train up a child in the way he should go, and when he is old he will not depart from it"   Proverbs 22:6 (KJV).

The phrase "train up" has three meanings in this verse:

1. dedication - the consistent meaning of the word as it appears throughout the Old Testament
2. instruction - how the word is used in Jewish writings
3. motivation - the meaning of the word in Aramaic

Train up a child, says the verse. There are seven Hebrew words for child. In this verse the word "child" is best translated as our word "dependent". As long as a child is dependent on his parents, he should receive training, regardless of his age. On an income tax form, you are asked to give the number of your dependents. At least the IRS understands that children are dependent on parents! Unfortunately, this can't be said of all parents. When does a child become independent? When he is no longer economically dependent on his parents.

We know most behavioral habits are formed in the first five years of life. Habits are difficult to change; therefore, the first five years of training are critical. This training not only includes discipline but learning to face consequences for disobedience. When your children are older, they'll remember their early childhood training. They'll have a reservoir of information to draw from. The parents responsibility is to fill this reservoir with the right information.

A Generation of Fixers

In today's society no one wants to face consequences for disobedience. Even in our court system criminals are given more consideration than victims. There are advocates for criminals' rights and there is much to-do about over crowding in prisons. But little emphasis is given to the fact that when you break the law, you have to suffer. Many parents have the means, either financially or through influence, to be "fixers." They don't want their children to suffer consequences; therefore, the tendency is to over protect them.

A man came for counseling whose son was in jail. He was desperate and needed our help. He told us about the times his son, as a teenager, had been caught shoplifting. Because this man was a prominent businessman and respected in his community, the store managers notified the father of his son's thefts. He paid for the merchandise and the charges were dropped. This went on for several years. The day before our appointment his son had gone to another city and had stolen an expensive car. He was caught and arrested. The police called and informed the father of the charges and told him his son was in the local jail. The people in this town didn't know the family and they had pressed charges.

The father had protected his son from the consequences of his illegal behavior again and again. Without the painful experience of consequences, the behavior continued.

"A foolish son is a grief to his father and bitterness to her who bore him"
Proverbs 17:25 (KJV).

"The rod and reproof give wisdom, but a child left undisciplined brings his mother to shame"
Proverbs 29:15 (AMP).

The Bible clearly says that punishment brings wisdom and without it a mother is brought to shame and a father grieves over his son.

The influential father who came to us for counsel is typical of today's generation of "fixers." This is a common pattern among people who are "controllers." Fathers and mothers who are "shakers and movers" in the business community are accustomed to fixing things as a means of controlling, and they continue the practice when they come home.

AA recommends a wise and practical saying in their handling of alcoholics, "Don't ever rob a man of his last drink." This father was constantly putting "soft cushions" under his son to soften the blows. If he had allowed his son to suffer the consequences of the shoplifting incidents, there is a strong possibility that the boy's behavior could have been altered and the car theft, arrest and jail prevented.

Speeding Sam

When Sam was a teenager, he got a speeding ticket. The ticket required that Sam appear in court. The judge knew Sam's father and called to offer to let Mr. Peeples pay the fine and exempt Sam from appearing in court. Sam's father wisely refused the offer. He wanted Sam to know what it was like to appear in court and face the judge. After almost forty-five years, Sam still remembers how he trembled as he stood before the judge waiting to hear the charges and amount of the fine. He was fined $20.00 (equivalent to about $80.00 today!) Sam had to pay the fine out of his own money. That was a lot of money to him then. It wasn't easy to turn loose of those hard-earned dollars; consequently, Sam drives very carefully through that area today and always checks his speed!

Too Much Stuffin'

So far we have talked about allowing our children to face the consequences of their own wrongdoing. But sometimes we have to face consequences that we aren't responsible for. They are simply the price we pay for living in a fallen world. These may be consequences caused by life's circumstances or injustice or hurt caused by other people. In our second chapter, "Understanding Your Child," we called these "shearing times," uncomfortable periods in our lives when we go through crises or difficult circumstances. Learning to face these consequences in a disciplined manner is just as important as facing consequences of our own making.

One morning I met my daughter, Dawn, at the grocery store. I was surprised to see that she had her ten-year-old son Mark with her. Normally Mark would have been in school that day. Dawn told me that Mark had a stomachache and was staying home. I left the grocery and prayed for Mark's stomach. While praying, I realized that Mark looked terrible. Not sick. Unhappy! I went to Dawn's house and invited Mark to come to the car for a talk.

"Mark, you look very unhappy," I began.

He said, "I'm not unhappy."

"You look unhappy to me. I know that at times you don't want to talk to your mom about your problems because you don't want to bother her."

Mark is a sensitive little boy who realizes how hard his mom works to support them. Several days before he had written her a note telling her that he was sorry her life had turned out this way and if she ever needed any money, she could go to his savings account and take out ten dollars.

As we continued to talk, I told him that if he could tell me about his problems, I would listen and try to help. His eyes filled with tears and his chin began to quiver.

"Meemaw," he confided, "some of the boys at school have teased me and hurt my feelings. I'm no good in baseball. I can't hit the ball and I can't run and I asked God to help me and He hasn't. I just don't understand why He won't help me. And I lost my backpack and I don't know what I did with it."

This was definitely a "time of shearing" for Mark. He had lost his friends, his confidence in God and his backpack all in one day!

Frankly, I wanted to cry with him, but I knew this wouldn't help him get through the day. He didn't need sympathy; he needed encouragement.

"Mark, you have two things to think about — you have your problems, and how your react to them. I would guess you get very angry when the boys tease you at school."

"No," he said. "I don't get angry. I just go play by myself."

"Why do you go play by yourself?" I asked.

"Because I don't like those boys."

"Well, I certainly wouldn't be surprised if you're angry at God because He didn't do what you asked Him to do."

He shrugged his shoulders. "I'm not angry, I just don't understand why He won't help me."

"Surely, you must be angry with yourself because you were careless with your backpack and you know your mother is going to have to buy another one and she doesn't have any money to waste." He was silent.

"Mark, you're just like your granddaddy!"

"How is he?"

"Well," I said, "when granddaddy gets mad, he just stuffs it."

He asked, "What does it mean to stuff it?"

I told him that it means you pretend you aren't mad when you really are. You ignore the angry feelings, but they just rumble around inside and sometimes give you a stomachache. He looked at me in shock! He was still crying, but you could see that he wanted to smile. A smile didn't seem appropriate for the moment.

"Mark, I can help you with your problems. We'll invite some boys over this summer and go swimming and cook hamburgers. Then you can make some friends. We'll ask Uncle Mark if he can help you with your baseball game. He's a good hitter and runner. I'll take you to school and we'll look for your backpack and if we can't find it, I'll get you another one."

I could help him with these disappointments, but I told him that I couldn't help him with his heart. I explained that his granddad had to learn to be honest about his reactions to people and situations. He had to admit that he got angry, and then ask God to forgive him. Granddaddy used to get stomachaches too from stuffing his anger until he learned the Bible verse in I John 1:9, "If we confess our sins, he is faithful and just to forgive us our sins, and to cleanse us from all unrighteousness" (KJV).

I explained this verse to Mark. "Confess" means to agree with God and "cleansed" means to be free from it. I asked him what he did when his mom called him in to dinner and his hands were dirty. He said he washed them. I asked him what happened to the dirt when he washed his hands. He looked at me as if I were kidding.

Mark said, "Meemaw, you know the dirt goes down the sink!"

I laughed and said, "Right. Now what do your hands look like?"

He answered, "They look clean."

I said, "Why do they look clean?"

I got the same look! In a most disgusted tone, Mark said they look clean because they *are* clean.

I laughed again. "You're right, Mark. When you confess your anger to God, He cleanses your heart. It's clean and can't make you sick anymore."

We prayed and went to see Uncle Mark; he agreed to spend Saturday working on baseball. We found the backpack. Several days later young Mark came rushing into our house to tell us that he had hit a home run and his run won the game. The coach held him up to the crowd and everyone clapped for him. Soon I saw some boys coming home to play after school.

Mark learned a great lesson. He learned that he couldn't keep from being disappointed (sheared), but he could do something about his reactions. He's one year older now and we're amazed at how well he handles disappointments. He has grown so much spiritually. He knows God can cleanse his heart and a clean heart feels better than an angry one!

"A glad heart makes a cheerful countenance, but by sorrow of heart the spirit is broken"   Proverbs 15:13 (AMP).

"All the days of the desponding and afflicted are made evil (by anxious thoughts and foreboding), but he who has a glad heart has a continual feast (regardless of circumstances)"   Proverbs 15:15 (AMP).

Sam and I know that our grandchildren will be hurt, disappointed, left out and laughed at some times. We can't prevent that from happening, but we can teach them to rely on the Lord and be strengthened instead of destroyed.

The consequences of Mark's stuffing his anger was a stomachache. The pain was so great he wasn't able to go to school that day. There was no medical reason for the pain, but the pain was very real.

"When I kept silence (before I confessed), my bones wasted away through my groaning all the day long"   Psalm 32:3 (AMP).

"Create in me a clean heart, O God; and renew a right, persevering and steadfast spirit within in me" 			*Psalm 51:10 (AMP).*

If you don't provide discipline and allow your children to face consequences, you assure them of harder times as adolescents and possibly for the rest of their lives.

Punishment

Consequences can result from physical pain due to emotional stress (as with our grandson, Mark) or as pain inflicted by a parent. The pain inflicted by a parent, we call punishment. Hold on! Patient, loving, kind, gentle parents inflict pain? Yes. It is exactly this type of parent — one who is "in shape" spiritually and emotionally — who is best able to administer punishment when it's needed.

Pain can be inflicted by a spanking, removing a privilege, denying a treat or adding a responsibility. Parents have to decide what works. Each child is different and should be handled differently. A child's age is a factor that should definitely be considered. As children get older, you'll need to change the privileges or treats to be denied. Periodically you'll need to evaluate what's important to your children.

When they're small, a good spank on the leg might work wonders. However, spanking might make another child more rebellious. You won't have much luck at all if you continue to spank a child as he becomes a teenager. At this stage, denials, confinement or adding responsibility are more effective. On the other hand, you might have a child who seems totally unaffected by any of these approaches!

That's the kind of child we had. Spanking had no effect on him. It never caused him to cry, repent or show the least bit of remorse! He just went about doing his own thing. We obviously had to resort to other forms of punishment. We tried denial. He never seemed to care when we took his bike away for the day or when we refused to let him play ball with the kids on the block. He was so creative, he always found something else he enjoyed doing.

One day we punished him by sending him to his room for one hour. He was so quiet, I wondered if he was still alive. I remember sneaking outside and peeking through the window to see what he was doing. He had taken a coat hanger from the closet, shaped it into a circle and hung it over the top of the closet door. Then he crumbled his notebook paper to form a ball. He was sitting on the foot of his bed practicing his basketball shots! Can you guess which child I am referring to?

I laugh now, but it wasn't funny that day. I was so disgusted because I couldn't find a way to punish Mark. Sam and I had to face the fact that nothing worked. We had one option left — do everything in our power to help Mark obey, which is why Mark required so much of our time. But we weren't willing to give up on him.

It Pays Off

Several months ago I spent the day with Mark. He said he was amazed at the discipline he received when he was growing up. He wondered how that happened since he remembered so well all the problems he had been through during those years.

I told him that his father and I had worked hard to help him do what we told him to do. I explained that we knew what we could make him do and we were aware of the things over which we had no control. Many, many times we helped him do what he didn't want to do. I reminded him that discipline is doing what is right when you don't want to. "As you were growing up," I reflected, "these habits were established little by little. Now they are paying off in your adult life."

Sam and I believe in punishment. There are times when it's absolutely necessary. Each situation must be evaluated as it comes. You, the parent, decide how many times you need to help a child obey. And you decide when the time has come to stop helping and use punishment. When you're certain that a child understands what he should or should not do, and he deliberately disobeys, that requires punishment.

"A youngster's heart is filled with rebellion, but punishment will drive it out of him"   Proverbs 22:15 (TLB)

Wrong Uses of Punishment

Punishment is necessary at times, but must be administered carefully. In an earlier chapter, we talked about how frustrated I became trying to change my children's attitudes through punishment, rather than dealing with their behavior. "Attitudes are God's business," Dr. Brandt told me. "God is the only one who can change a person's heart and He does this when someone asks Him through prayer." Punishment should always be directed toward changing behavior, not attitudes.

I've shared this with many parents and most of them have resisted just as I did. I spoke recently with a young mother who had been spanking her little girl for a bad attitude. She said she thought I was wrong, but just for fun she would give it a try. She called me on the telephone several weeks later to report that a miracle had taken place.

This little six-year-old would scream when she didn't get her way. I suggested that this mom ignore her tantrums. She said the noise was too great to ignore. I suggested that she put her in her room and tell her the screams hurt her ears, close the door and walk away. She did what I said and the child stopped screaming. She was a smart six-year-old. Why scream when it didn't bother anyone? That was useless, and even this child knew better than to do something useless!

I can remember years ago when my mother often said, "Sit up in that chair and wipe that smirk off your face!" Oh. . . did that make me mad! I sat up and wiped the smirk off my face, but I was still smirking on the inside. I knew better than to cross my mother, but even then I knew she couldn't make me stop smirking in my heart. She could make me appear to change, but I took pride in the fact that she couldn't make me really change! I had a bad attitude and my mother couldn't do anything about it.

I was raised in the generation that learned to be a fake, especially in the southern part of the United States. We were raised to "act nice"! It didn't seem to matter if it was just an act.

When invited to parties, I was told to act nice. I was a reflection of my mother's training and she didn't want my behavior to embarrass her. However, learning to act nice taught me to be a hypocrite. The word *hypocrite* is a Greek term which refers to a classical actor in the Greek theater. Instead of grease paint, a mask was made to portray the character. When the actor put on the mask, he had two faces, the one the public saw and the real one underneath. Hence, a hypocrite is someone with two faces. The strongest words Jesus spoke were directed to hypocrites whose pretense offended him deeply.

Be careful that you don't force your children to wear two faces. Don't punish them for the way they look at you. This will force them to look at you the way they think you want you them to look. Give your children the freedom to be who they are. Then you'll know what they are really thinking and feeling.

Punish your children for willful disobedience, but not for a bad attitude. In other words, punish them for what they do wrong, not for what is going on inside them. As Dr. Brandt warned, don't meddle in God's business. Don't invade His territory. Take care of what your children *do* and pray that they will let God take care of *how* they do it!

A Final Help

We've discovered another aspect of using punishment wisely that has helped us greatly. Use a different type of punishment for each act of disobedience. If the punishment is going to be taking away a privilege or treat, study your children to know which privileges or treats are important to them. Then rank these in order of importance. If a child needs to be punished, choose the least important treat or privilege to take away first. If that isn't effective, move to the next most important privilege, and so on.

Increasing the pressure this way can have significant effects. Use the least important for a while, and then move to the next most important. Be careful not to move too fast or you will loose the effectiveness of increasing the pressure. Many parents act impulsively in anger and impose the most severe penalty first, thus losing the opportunity to increase the pressure. We urge you to evaluate your own spirit before you choose which form of punishment is appropriate for your child.

Discipline: The Proof of Love

Becoming a good disciplinarian will result in your having a strong sense of well being. You can be content in knowing you are doing what is right, regardless of what is going on around you. Don't be caught in the trap of protecting children from the consequences of their disobedience; know the difference between discipline and punishment and use each wisely; take advantage of increasing the pressure. Using a combination of these principles can significantly increase your effectiveness in parenting.

Disciplining our children, the Bible says, is a measure of how much we love them.

"For whom the Lord loves He corrects, even as a father corrects the son in whom he delights" Proverbs 3:12 (AMP).

"If you refuse to discipline your son, it proves you don't love him; for if you love him you will be prompt to punish him" Proverbs 13:24 (TLB).

Lack of discipline and punishment is one of the major factors in the breakdown of modern society — which is evident in this list of staggering statistics taken from the Children's Defense Fund.

Every sixty minutes in America:
125 young people see their parents get divorced.
107 children are born out of wedlock.
137 children run away from home.
77 children are abused and neglected.
66 teenagers drop out of school.
18 teens are arrested for drinking or drunken driving.
9 teenagers are arrested for drug abuse.
117 teens (women under 20) get pregnant.
323 teenagers become sexually active.
46 teenagers have abortions.
26 teenagers contract syphilis or gonorrhea.
1 teenager commits suicide.

These are heartbreaking facts, reflecting a lot of hurt and hardship. Obviously, it is important to discipline children so they grow up to be responsible members of society, but perhaps even more important to you now is how much discipline plays a role in developing a positive self-image in your child.

One of the most talked about subjects in America these days is self-image. Parents become anxious when they realize that their child may be developing a poor self-image or suffers from low self-esteem. In the next chapter we'll explore the direct relationship between discipline and self-esteem.

CHAPTER **6**

BUILDING A
GOOD SELF-IMAGE

CHAPTER VI

Building A Good Self-Image

"He that refuseth instruction despiseth his own soul: but he that heareth reproof getteth understanding."

Proverbs 15:32 (KJV)

"He that getteth wisdom loveth his own soul; he that keepeth understanding shall find good."

Proverbs 19:8 (KJV)

In an earlier chapter, we told the story of a couple who sought counseling for their rebellious son who had "acute temper tantrums" when things didn't go his way. As their normally cooperative thirteen-year-old became more rebellious, showing a marked change of behavior, the father had been most alarmed by his son's temper tantrums. Sue, the boy's mother, was most concerned about her son's depreciating self-worth.

As they described their son's behavior, these anxious parents described an unruly teenager who was challenging and refusing instruction. How would you define a rebel? Isn't it someone who refuses instruction? It should be no surprise then, that rebels have poor self-images.

Lower the Standard?

As most parents come to realize that rebellion leads to a poor self-image, they try to solve the problem by giving their children fewer rules to rebel against. In an effort to restore their children's self-image at any cost, they often remove or reduce their standards. But rules don't cause rebellion, they reveal it. Parents are disappointed when relaxing the rules doesn't improve their children's self-image. They are left wondering, "Now what do we do?"

This was the question the parents of the thirteen-year-old rebellious teenager were asking. Sam counseled these parents to maintain an authoritative stand, rather than indulging their son's waywardness. Sam was confident in his counsel because of the above verses which speak clearly and directly to the problem. He asked both parents to read and reflect on Proverbs 15:32. Sam explained that the King James phrase "despiseth his own soul" can best be understood in modern terms as "has a poor self-image," "low self-esteem," "no self respect," or "not liking oneself." They could easily identify with this explanation.

Suddenly they understood the cause of their son's low self-worth. He had been refusing instruction, not doing what he was told to do, and he had lost respect for himself. As we counsel parents, Sam and I are often asked, "What instruction do you mean?" Instruction includes directions from the Bible, parents, teachers, civil authorities or anyone who has rightful authority over us.

Surprised and Relieved!

If refusing instruction is the problem, how do you solve it? The answer is found in Proverbs 19:8, our second verse, "He that getteth wisdom loveth his own soul." Notice the contrast in the two verses. In the first, "He *despiseth* his own soul" and in the second, "He *loveth* his own soul." We would substitute "loveth his own soul" with the phrase "has a good self-image," "high self- esteem," "self-respect," or "likes himself."

Sue asked Sam to explain the term, "getting wisdom." Because Sam had done a lengthy word study on the word "wisdom," he was able to provide a simple, yet satisfactory answer. The word wisdom in its most practical sense here means "knowledge experienced."

Wisdom goes beyond knowledge or knowing what to do. It means that knowledge must be put into practice and become a part of one's experience. Sam told Sue that her son's self-esteem would improve when he did two things: 1) stopped refusing instruction, and 2) started heeding his parents' instructions and making them part of his experience.

Sue looked surprised and relieved. Sam understood why she was surprised. She, like so many parents, had been led to believe that having a poor self-image is a very complicated problem. Obviously, a complicated problem calls for a complicated solution.

Sue was relieved because as a Christian she believed the Bible and was willing to accept what it said. Popular thinking would have us believe that the environment and poor parenting cause a child to have a poor self-image. Yes, she said, that's what she thought.

Truth Sets us Free

We don't deny that these are strong influences in a child's life, but hope comes when we accept the truth. When Sue understood and accepted the truth, her guilty feelings about her son's poor self-image began to fade. This was also why she felt relieved. The truth had set her free! It amazes us how accurately the Bible can diagnose and pre-scribe solutions for people's problems, giving them hope and clear direction. This mother left our office confident that she could help her son overcome his problem of a poor self-image. It was a simple matter of making sure that he did what she told him to do!

We have two options to choose from when seeking help for our-selves or our children. The most popular option is the secular teaching based on humanism. Sigmund Freud is considered the founder of modern psychotherapy and the leading proponent of this thinking. He spent hours obtaining case histories to determine the background of his patients. He hoped to be able to place the blame for their problem on the environment, the circumstances or the way people had treated his patients. In other words, he wanted to transfer the blame.

Being able to transfer the blame allows you to place the blame out-side yourself, but it doesn't eliminate the problem. You learn to live with the problem when the problem results from someone else's behavior. You can develop "coping skills," but the problem is still there.

While secularism teaches you to look outside yourself for causes, the Bible teaches you to look inside yourself. A person's self-image is the direct result of what that person thinks about himself. The word *self*, as defined in Webster's, means "the identity of a person" and *image* means "a picture or a reflection." Self-image means "the picture you have of yourself."

"The way to gain a good reputation is to endeavor to be what you desire to appear."

Socrates

What's the Plumb line?

You decide which option you want to follow: secular or biblical. This will determine your guidelines. These guidelines serve as your plumb line. Do you know what a plumb line is? It's a line you follow in order to keep things straight! Once you deviate from the plumb line, things become more and more "out of line."

I wanted to wallpaper my kitchen and I didn't have enough money to hire someone to do the job. So I found a discount wallpaper store and found just the right paper. One day while sitting at the kitchen table, Dawn and I decided we would hang the paper. It was prepasted, so all we had to do was measure the wall correctly, cut the paper and wet the back side. We jumped up from the table, got the yard stick and began measuring the wall. We decided the best place to start was in the corner, then simply work our way around the kitchen.

We had fun hanging the paper. I remember the laughter and our plans to go into the paper-hanging business. The kitchen was small so we finished in about four hours.

After we were all done, Dawn and I stood back to admire our handiwork. Dawn began to laugh and I began to cry. The paper was a striped pattern. Because the room wasn't square, each stripe leaned more and more to the right. What a mess we'd made! I dried my eyes and decided to simply cut the legs off one side of all my chairs. When we sat at the table in those lopsided chairs, the paper would be straight!

Cut Off the Legs?

Needless to say, I didn't really cut the legs off the chairs. I just had to live with the leaning stripes on the wallpaper. I learned to cope. What did we do wrong? We failed to use a plumb line.

How simple it would have been for me to tack a nail in the ceiling and tie a string to the nail. The string would have hung straight and we could have followed that string to hang the paper in a beautiful pattern. A simple mistake caused a lot of distress!

As we seek to help our children develop a positive self-image, we need to follow an unswerving plumb line. God has provided that line in his Word. It's a simple line. One line will do, "He who refuseth instruction, despiseth his own soul..."

We trust you will choose to use the Bible as your plumb line. Bible verses that offer promises have conditions attached to them. The condition in these promise verses is to quit refusing instruction and begin doing what you know you should do. If you do this, the verse promises that you'll have a good self-image. Unfortunately, we tend to focus on the promise and look for ways to get results through a means other than the conditions given in the Bible. It seems to us that the focus should be on *our* responsibility (the conditions).

Reasons for Low Self-Worth

According to a recent Gallup Poll, many of us are concerned about low self-worth. One-third of Americans, the poll showed, suffer from low self-esteem. As Christian counselors we have found this is true of Christians too. These are the most common reasons we are given for a poor self-image:

1) My parents put me down.
2) I had an older sister who always did things better than me.
3) I have no self-respect because my husband left me.
4) I'm overweight.
5) I never had a good friend.
6) I don't like the way my hair looks.
7) My classmates always made fun of me.
8) I could never hit the ball well enough to please my father.

What happens when your parents put you down? We often feel resentful. What happens when your sister does things better than you and always gets the praise you yearn for? This can cause jealousy. What happens when your husband leaves you for another woman? Most women become bitter and jealous. Do you get the point? When things don't go our way, it's human to become resentful and bitter. It's human to burn with jealousy. The Bible teaches that man's nature is fallen, and therefore prone to sin. Sin is in man's heart. When something doesn't go our way, a sinful reaction can easily come out of our hearts. Would you respect someone who was angry, hostile, bitter, jealous, etc.? If your answer is no, then why would you respect yourself when you harbor these feelings in your own heart?

When people tell us, "I don't like myself," we ask what there is about themselves that they don't like? Seems too simple, doesn't it? They look at us in a strange way. The typical response is, "You still don't understand." Then they begin to repeat their stories, complaining about what someone has said about them or done to them.

Now comes the difficult task for us as counselors. We must try to convey the biblical perspective. It's not what has happened to you, we advise, that causes you to have a poor self-image; it's how you respond to what happens.

Read what Jesus says in Mark 7:14-23. Our familiar paraphrase of this verse is:

> *The circumstances of life,*
> *The events of life,*
> *The people around me in life,*
> *Do not make me the way I am*
> *But reveal the way I am.*

The shortest way to summarize this is in Jesus's words in John 14:1a: "Let not your heart be troubled..." If your heart is troubled, who let it become anxious? If you let it, you can "unlet" it? If someone else let it, you will probably try to force them to "unlet" it! We tend to put pressure on others to change so that *our* hearts will not be troubled.

How do we "let" our hearts be troubled? More often than not, we allow sin to accumulate inside our hearts. Sin has troubling effects, one of which is a poor self-image.

It's My Background!

As we've said, it's commonly believed and taught that a damaging environment while growing up is the major cause of low self-esteem. We agree that it is painful to grow up in an environment where you are mistreated. We have great sympathy for those who have been constantly mistreated. This sympathy drives us to want to help you understand the truth so you can be free!

We often meet with resistance because this is a new and different approach to many people. But as you accept this truth, you'll want to change the way you think. Change can be difficult, and is sometimes frightening. However, resistance should never cause us to back away from truth. Don't let resistance cause you to adjust the plumb line. Adherence to the plumb line keeps us straight.

To refuse biblical instruction robs us of a positive self-image. And we are told to keep our hearts clean. When we fail to do either of these things, we rebel against God. To be free of sin, God instructs us: "If we confess our sins, he is faithful and just, and will forgive our sins and cleanse us from all unrighteousness" I John 1:9 (RSV). Notice you have to confess YOUR sin, not your parent's sin, your older sister's sin, your husband's sin, or your classmate's sin.

If you're wondering why we use I John 1:9 so often, it's because we need it so often!

Confessing your sin makes your heart clean and empty. It's good to have a clean heart, but it's risky to leave it empty! After cleansing your heart, ask the Lord to fill it with love, joy, peace, patience, forgiveness, gentleness, kindness, and self control. With those qualities in your heart, why wouldn't you like yourself? Those qualities naturally produce a positive self-image and high self-esteem.

Now do you see the importance of using a biblical approach to helping someone improve their self-worth? It's impossible for us to change our own hearts or the hearts of other people. It's God's business to change hearts.

How simple and practical the Bible is as it speaks to life's basic needs. Once a friend said, "It's amazing how complicated the Bible can be when you don't want to do what it says." It is good to remember that God's Word is the word of the Creator giving instructions to those He created. What a shame that this profound book is ignored or is often the last resort, even for Christians.

Buying a Poor Self-Image

There are many subtle ways parents can inadvertently contribute to a child's poor self-image. Ruth and Joe were well-meaning parents who illustrate this. Their son was single, in his late twenties and out of work. Randy had approached his parents twice before asking for money. As concerned parents, Ruth and Joe had given him the money he wanted. The second time Randy came to them, they decided they wouldn't help him financially again. They gave him enough money to live on for the next three months. In their minds, this was enough time for him to find a job and begin supporting himself. At the end of the three months, he was back on their doorstep, still unemployed. His

parents asked what he had done with the money they had given him. They were amazed by how frivolously he had spent it. They asked if he had looked for employment. He had made very few efforts to find a job.

Randy said he just didn't feel good about himself when he interviewed for jobs. His self-image was so poor, his parents understood why employers wouldn't hire him. If only he could get a job and be successful, they thought, he would feel good about himself.

During a counseling session, Ruth and Joe told Sam that they had told Randy that they wouldn't help him financially again. But now he was out of food, his rent was due, he had no gas for his car and he was still unemployed. Ruth and Joe had discussed this at length, wondering if they should help him again. They weren't in disagreement with each other, but they were unsure about what to do.

Sam said the immediate goal was for Randy to get a job. They agreed. Sam asked what they felt was the greatest thing that prevented Randy from getting a job. They replied, "his poor self image." What a dilemma! The very thing that Randy hoped to get from a job — a positive self-image — was what he needed in order to get a job.

Sam told Ruth and Joe that Randy needed to deal with his rebellious spirit and decide to cooperate with his parents by following their instructions. Explaining Proverbs 15:32, Sam said that because Randy was refusing their instruction, it wasn't surprising that he had a poor self-image. "By continuing to give him money," Sam pointed out, "you're buying your child a poor self-image."

They were stunned. They hadn't realized what they were doing. "Now we know exactly what to do," they said. "We can't give Randy any more money!"

Because these parents had biblical direction, they had hope for the future. Their hope didn't rest in Randy's choices, but in the confidence that they had made the right decision. It was clear that they needed to stop rewarding Randy's bad behavior. By continuing to give him money, they were helping him perpetuate failure.

It is worth mentioning here that sometimes we assume that self-confidence and a positive self-image mean the same thing. The following definitions will help you see the difference:

Confidence is the realization that you are equipped with the skills to perform a task.

Good self-image occurs when you are not violating the dictates of your conscience.

If Randy decided to start doing what he knew he should do, he would develop a good self-image. If he took a job in a field in which he had never worked, however, he might still lack confidence. But as he trained and acquired skills to perform the job, gradually he would become self-confident. Randy could have a positive self-image while he was building self-confidence. Self-confidence has to do with training skills and experience. Self-image has to do with moral conscience.

Loving Ourselves

It is common for people who have a poor self-image to be withdrawn. They have trouble looking you in the eye. They usually hang their heads, and prefer to be alone most of the time. When children act this way, parents want to push them out of their bedrooms where they seek solitude. Anxious parents usually think the answer to the problem of withdrawal is to force a child to socialize with friends. But withdrawal isn't the problem; it is only a symptom of the problem.

What is the problem? Your son or daughter doesn't like anyone. How are you going to get your child to like other people? To solve the problem, you must get to the root of the problem, and deal with it. In Matthew 22:36-40, Jesus was asked, "Teacher, which is the greatest commandment in the law?" Jesus said, "You shall love the Lord your God with all your heart, and with all your soul, and with all your

mind. This is the great and first commandment. And a second is like
it, You shall love your neighbor as yourself. On these two commandments depend all the law and the prophets" (RSV).

What could this possibly have to do with solving the problem of
withdrawal! Let us show you. In these verses, God establishes our priorities. We are to love: 1) God, 2) ourselves, and then 3) our neighbors.

Usually we think of loving our neighbor before we love ourselves.
We have the idea that it is selfish to love ourselves before our neighbors. The key word in this verse is the little word, "as." It means "like,
similar, in like manner." So we are to love our neighbor like, similar,
in like manner as we love ourselves. However, if you don't love yourself, how can you love your neighbor? Neighbors include your friends.
When you love your friends, you don't withdraw from them. We seek
out those we love. If your child loves his friends, you won't have to
force him to be with them and enjoy them.

The self-love we're talking about has nothing to do with narcissism,
egoism or selfishness. We are content and love ourselves when our
conscience is clear, we are at peace with ourselves, when we know we
have done what is right and have nothing to hide.

Jonathan Edwards said it clearly, "...to keep clear of concealment, to
keep clear of the need of concealment, to do nothing he might not do
on the Boston Common at noonday. I cannot say how more and more
that seems to me to be the glory of a young man's life. It is an awful
hour when the first necessity of hiding anything comes. The whole life
is different after that. When there are questions to be feared and eyes
to be avoided and subjects which must not be touched, then the bloom
of life is gone."

If you have a poor self-image, it is difficult or impossible to keep
the great commandment Jesus gave. Those living in disobedience usually have difficulty loving God. And disobedience, as we've said, leads
to a poor self-image which keeps you from loving your neighbor. If
you don't love yourself, you won't be able to love God or your neighbor either. You become your own roadblock to obeying what Jesus
said is the greatest commandment of all!

The Apostle Paul stressed this too as he taught about interpersonal
relationships. In Galatians 5:14 he says, quoting Jesus, "For all the law
is fulfilled in one word, even in this; Thy shalt love thy neighbor as
thyself."

Just imagine, we keep the entire law of God when we love our
neighbor as we love ourselves. Parents need to realize the implications

of this truth. Having a positive self-image is a key factor in your child's social development.

Be careful not to fall into the trap of common secular thinking, and don't stumble over the simplicity of the biblical approach. Be willing to take this basic principle of truth, "He that getteth wisdom loveth his own soul. . ." and give it broad application.

Parents should provide a supportive environment for their children by encouraging them and helping them to be obedient. . . "getting wisdom." We defined wisdom as knowledge experienced. When you help children obey, you not only establish discipline in them, but you also nurture a strong sense of self-worth, which enables them to love God, themselves and others.

The better you know your child, the more you can help him/her become a happy, well-adjusted individual. A key to this kind of understanding comes as you begin to unravel the mystery of your son or daughter's personality, the subject of our next chapter.

CHAPTER 7

PERSONALITY
DIFFERENCES

MAKE
A
DIFFERENCE

CHAPTER VII

Personality Differences — Make A Difference

"Train up a child in the way he should go (and in keeping with his individual gift or bent) and when he is old he will not depart from it."
Proverbs 22:6 (AMP)

As we "train up our children," it is helpful to understand their unique personalities. Children are different. Some are emotional, others more analytical; some love to socialize, others enjoy being alone. One type of personality is not better than another, they're just different.

It is important to realize that one's personality type is not an excuse for anything. When your child is disobedient, this has nothing to do with their personality. All personality types can choose to be obedient or disobedient. However the *way* in which they are disobedient can vary according to their personality type. Don't forget that harmony between family members will exist when each decides to deal with their sin by confessing it, yeilding to the Holy Spirit's control and walking in the Spirit.

Being able to identify and understand your and your child's personality type will explain how and why you are different.

In our family we mislabeled one of our children wrong when he was only different. We had trouble understanding his way of thinking and doing things. On many occasions we got angry and frustrated with him because he didn't think and do things the way we did. We then labeled him wrong, blind to the possibility that instead of being wrong he could be different. This also caused him to be frustrated.

As parents and as counselors we've learned that respecting and appreciating different personality types, as you walk in the Spirit, goes a long way toward improving family relationships — between parents and children and mom and dad as well.

Personality and Personality Differences

It's amazing how often we use the term *personality* and yet don't know what it really means. Webster defines personality as, "That which constitutes an individual as a distinct person, or that which constitutes individuality."

If personality gives us our individuality, then it must have integrated into it those things which distinguish us one from another. What are these things? They can be differences in the most fundamental parts of who we are. Psychologists through the centuries have studied and observed people to isolate some of these basic, and at the same time, common differences.

Carl Jung did this. He was one of first people to develop a theory about personality types. In the 1950s, a mother-daughter team, Katharine Briggs and Isabel Myers expanded on Jung's theory and developed a tool to help people identify their personality type. This instrument is called the Myers-Briggs Type Indicator or MBTI® — the most widely used personality assessment in the world.

Most people who have studied personalities agree that we are predisposed to our personality traits, in other words, they are with us from birth. The proverb states that we should train up our child in keeping with his individual "gift or bent." An important part of that gift or bent is his personality. Parents need to know and understand the strengths and weaknesses of their child if they are going to obey what the proverb says. One of the most helpful ways to identify these strengths and weaknesses is to understand personality types. This will enable you to better train your child in keeping with his gift or bent.

Personality and Character

Understanding the word *character* also sheds light on the uniqueness of children. Webster defines character as, "The peculiar qualities, impressed by nature or habit on a person, which distinguishes him from others; these constitute real character, and the qualities which he is supposed to possess, constitute his estimated character or reputation. Hence we say a character is not formed when the person has not acquired stable and distinctive qualities."

How do personality and character relate to each other? The following description, which we've developed, has helped us understand and explain the relationship:

Our personality is the vehicle through which our character is made known (manifest or expressed).

It has been said that, "We are attracted to individuals because of their personality, but after that we have to live with their character."

How your character traits are made known to others will depend upon your personality type. How other's character traits are manifested will depend upon their personality type. Before you judge someone's character traits, whether they be strong or weak, remember to factor in personality differences. This will greatly influence your judgment.

As Christians, character is the part of our make-up that God is very interested in changing and improving. His purpose is to conform us to the image of His Son (Romans 8:28,29). The character traits of our Lord are those He wants to develop in us: love, joy, peace, patience, kindness, goodness, faithfulness, gentleness and self-control (Galatians 5:22,23).

There are also negative or sinful character traits which we need to ask the Lord to forgive and cleanse us from each time we act or react unrighteously. We should allow Him to make them less and less a part of our experience. These may be anger, jealousy, selfishness, immorality, indecency, deceit, covetousness or envy (Galatians 5:19,20 and Mark 7:21,22).

Some wrongs *are* wrongs; they are truly not differences. We call these "character flaws." It is important to distinguish between personality traits and character flaws. It's not unusual for a child (and parents as well) to try and "sweep a character flaw under the personality type rug." Personality types are not excuses for anything!

A mother and father had come for counseling with their two teenage children to try and improve their family relationships. Each of them took the Myers-Briggs Type Indicator assessment and had received their reports. After reviewing them, the son turned to his dad and said, "Now you understand why I can't get home at 11:30 at night!"

The boy smiled with great relief. The father turned to Sam with an anguished, searching look and said, "Could this be true?"

Sam shook his head. "I'm sorry, son, but you're talking about a character flaw." He explained that ALL personality types can decide to be home on time. The son's smug smile turned to a look of disappointment. His father was relieved.

Understanding Differences

Before we try to understand our children, we often need to understand ourselves better. In this chapter, we'll explore what we mean by differences in personalities and you'll have a chance to identify your own personality type, then apply what you've learned to other family members.

There are no right or wrong personality types. No one type is better or worse than the other.

The MBTI Personality Type theory is based on four basic mental functions that we all routinely use in living out each day. The four functions are:

1. Energy source - where you get your energy
2. Perceiving - taking in information
3. Judging - making decisions with the information
4. Outer world living - how you handle the world around you

Each of these functions has two choices, referred to as preferences. We all have a distinct "preference" for ways of thinking and doing things.

Doing What Comes Naturally

The word *preference* is key to understanding personality type. To demonstrate the idea of preferences, try the following task.

Take a pen or pencil and a piece of paper, then write out your name just as if you were signing a check. Now place the pen or pencil in your other hand and sign your name again below the other signature.

The hand you used for your first signature is your preferred hand. The other hand is your non-preferred hand. Comparing the two exercises, this should describe what happened:

1. For the first signature:
   a. You didn't make a conscious decision about which hand to use
   b. No conscious thought was required
   c. The task was accomplished with ease
   d. Very little time was involved

2. For the second signature:
   a. A conscious effort and concentration were required
   b. The task seemed awkward and uncomfortable
   c. Required more time to complete the task

Just as you prefer one hand over the other, so you will prefer one of the choices of each personality function. One is preferred, the other non-preferred. That is, you feel more comfortable and confident doing things one way or another. Simplicity is the essence of all things profound! The premise for personality type theory is simple but the understanding and use of it is profound. We are information processors. Most of the time we are not aware that we are doing this. First, we are constantly perceiving or taking in information. Secondly, we are making decisions with that information. We may act on it immediately or store it for future reference.

This is at the "heart" of our personality. These two parts of processing information are represented by the second and third function.

What Are Your Preferences?

Let's take a simplified personality assessment based on the four functions described earlier. As you read the descriptions below, you should be able to identify with one preference more than the other. Write down the letter of your preference in each of the four functions. At the end of the exercise, you should have four letters. This combination represents your personality type. Some of the possible combinations are: ISTJ, ENFP, ESTJ, INTP, etc.

By making various combinations of these eight preferences, we arrive at sixteen personality types. Let us remind you again that they represent combinations of preferences. Your personality includes some of all eight. But you've used four of these more throughout your life than the other four. Therefore, your natural tendency is to use the preferred four — just like your preferred hand. But don't forget that you were able to write with your non-preferred hand too!

Let's paint a personality portrait of who you are.

Introversion   vs   Extraversion

First, ask yourself what energizes you. Extraverts tend to draw their energy from people; whereas, introverts usually seek solitude to recharge their batteries. Extraversion is abbreviated by the letter E, and introversion by I. Some characteristics of both type are given below.

Those who prefer Extraversion (E):
1. Get energy from being around people, things and events
2. Interaction with people is important
3. Are involved
4. Energy is usually expended outwardly
5. Have a broad range of interests
6. Often speak without thinking

Those who prefer Introversion (I):
1. Get energy from within themselves
2. Need and enjoy contemplation
3. Value peace and privacy
4. Usually expend energy inwardly
5. Have a narrow range of interests
6. Are self-motivated and self-reinforcing
7. By comparison, they are more shy and cautious
8. Often think without speaking

Sensing   vs   Intuition

The next function describes the way we take in information. A person who has a preference for Sensing (S) depends on and feels comfortable with information taken in through the five senses. One who has a preference for Intuition (N) depends on that "sixth sense" we call intuition. Which do you prefer?

Those who prefer Sensing (S):
1. See things as they are
2. Like and trust facts
3. Have a goal of being realistic
4. Value what has been learned from the past
5. Tend to be practical and sensible
6. Characterized more by perspiration, than inspiration

Those who prefer Intuition (N):
1. See things by way of insight
2. See things as they could be
3. Value different and new experiences
4. Have a well-developed imagination and trust it
5. Characterized more by inspiration, than perspiration

Thinking   vs   Feeling

The third function focuses on the way we make decisions with the information we receive. Again, there are two preferences: Thinking (T) and Feeling (F). Which preference best describes you?

Those who prefer Thinking (T):
1. Are more objective, than subjective
2. When asked to prioritize truthfulness and tactfulness, would choose truthfulness
3. Require and are comfortable with using logical principles

Those who prefer Feeling (F):
1. Are more subjective, than objective
2. Give priority to tactfulness over truthfulness
3. Use values in decision-making
4. Are concerned about how others might feel and what they will say to others as a decision or opinion is announced
5. Value harmony in decision-making

Judging   vs   Perceiving

The fourth function deals with the way we choose to live in our outer world. Are you a Judging (J) or Perceiving (P) person?

Those who prefer Judging (J):

1. Enjoy and feel confident in the decision-making process
2. Desire early closure
3. Comfortable with decisions once they're made and can move on to the next project
4. Rely on encouragement and acceptance from others
5. Quickly organize what is observed
6. Work-play-work people, who don't enjoy leisure time as much when there is work remaining to be done

Those who prefer Perceiving (P):

1. Enjoy and are patient in collecting information
2. Comfortable when thinking and observing the world around them
3. Prefer delayed closure
4. Are often uncomfortable about a decision once it's made and are often slow to move to the next project
5. Play-work-play people enjoy leisure time more because they aren't worrying about the work remaining to be done

As you made your choices, you now have four letters representing your personality type. (This has been a short assessment. A more accurate assessment can be made by using the standard MBTI instrument.) Your personality types may differ in at least one or two letters. Possibly even three, or maybe even four! If you aren't aware of these differences and ignore them, this can lead to problems as Sam and I discovered. On the other hand, learning to appreciate these differences can bring new harmony in your home.

Appreciating Differences

When Sam first took the Myers-Briggs Type Indicator assessment and learned about his personality type, he was amazed by how accurate the description was. I read his report and had the same reaction. I immediately took the assessment too and benefited greatly from what I learned about myself. So did Sam.

Sam's personality type is ISTJ. I'm a ESTJ. You'll notice that there is only one letter that is different in the four letters. But what a difference that one letter can make!

Sam practiced dentistry for sixteen years. After a long, hard day at the office, he would come home exhausted. When he came home, he typically greeted the family, then immediately sat down in his easy chair and read the newspaper. I wondered why he didn't come into the kitchen and chat with me as I got the dinner ready.

"What's wrong with him?" I thought. "What have I done now? Why is he mad at me?"

Since he wouldn't come into the kitchen, I decided to join him in the living room. When I sat down and talked, he tried to listen while continuing to read the paper.

Realizing that Sam wasn't paying attention, I would storm out of the room. "I wonder what's wrong with her?" Sam thought. "What have I done? Why is she mad with me? Can't I have some peace and quiet for a few minutes to read the paper?"

I had been home taking care of three small children. At the end of the day, I looked forward to Sam's coming home so I could have some adult conversation. I had quite a few things to talk about!

Sam had been at the office dealing with people all day. He could hardly wait to get away from people and their problems to relax at home, enjoying some much-needed peace and privacy.

Both of our "batteries" had run low. I needed to be energized with some adult conversation. Sam needed to be energized with some quiet

time. For most of our thirty-eight years of marriage, we didn't understand why we were different. We just learned to cope with each other.

When we became Christians we became more caring and accepting
which affected our inter-personal relationships. But now we understand our differences. With this information, we've learned to respect
each other's needs and cooperate to meet those needs. Sam has to
enter into some conversation and I have to be willing to let him "have
his space." Having this information when we got married, could have
saved alot of trouble! You can benefit from this information. You don't
need to struggle like we did.

The personality type information is useful but we must have a spirit
of cooperation. Then the information blended with a coorperative spirit will provide harmony in our relationships. This information is useful in the hands of a Spirit-filled Christian. Otherwise it could be used
against each other.

The extravert in our house starts to get energized early in the morning. Before Sam leaves for the office, I'm on the phone charging my
batteries. Sometimes I'm into my second call as I wave good-by to
him. Can you believe that Sam doesn't care if he doesn't talk on the
phone all morning! He can even sit alone in his office for an entire
morning and feel great!

Wrong Labels

Sam expected Mark to be like him. This turned out to be a great hin-
drance as Sam tried to build a good relationship with our son. A part
of Mark's personality is different from his dad's: the difference partic-
ularly shows up in the way Mark carries out responsibilities.

For example, one of Mark's responsibilities when he was growing up was to cut the grass and wash the car on Saturdays. On Friday evenings Sam would remind Mark that tomorrow was the day to do these chores. One Saturday morning at 8:00 Mark's friend pulled up in front of the house and blew the car horn. Mark grabbed his golf clubs and ran out the door. Sam ran to the door and yelled as the car drove away, "Mark, what about the grass and the car?" Mark waved as the car turned the corner. Sam was furious.

"When will he learn to do what I ask him to do?" he thought to himself. "Will he ever take his responsibilities seriously? How can he possibly enjoy his golf game knowing that he hasn't cut the grass or washed the car?" And the final judgment: "He'll never be able to keep a job."

Mark came home at 3:00 that afternoon. He cut the grass and washed the car. Mark sensed that his dad was unhappy with him. He wondered why. Didn't he cut the grass and wash the car as he was supposed to?

Let's examine the scene. Sam didn't tell Mark WHEN on Saturday he should wash the car and cut the grass. Sam thought to himself, "After all, that wasn't necessary. Doesn't everyone do their chores before they play? Of course! At least anyone who is normal and has any sense of responsibility." Sam worried all day about his irresponsible, disobedient, "wrong" son.

Was Mark wrong or different? Obviously, he *was* and *is* different. If Sam had told Mark to do his chores BEFORE he played golf, he would have disobeyed and been wrong. Sam mislabeled Mark unfairly because he naturally assumed that everyone handled their responsibilities the way he did.

This story is not to imply that Mark didn't disobey on occasion. Nor did we excuse his disobedience because of the difference in our personality types.

The Value of Self-Awareness

The primary benefit of knowing your personality type is self-awareness. Self-awareness helps you understand why you function in life as you do. As you understand yourself better you can appreciate the strengths of the preferred parts of your personality and use them more wisely in relationships, in assigning or accepting tasks and even in career selection. You'll also begin to understand the differences between yourself and other people. Again, we repeat: there are no right or wrong, bad or good personality types. Knowing this makes it easier to accept others and their differences.

Just as you can make an educated guess about the four letters that characterize your mate's personality, you can also make an educated guess about your child's four letters. There are probably some differences between you and your child, and you'll benefit from being aware of the differences just as we benefited from understanding Mark's personality type. Richard's parents discovered this too.

Richard's mother sat in our counseling office and described her problem. Richard was a sophomore in college, taking pre-med courses. The year was ending and his grades for the past two years were poor, definitely not good enough to get into medical school. Richard's father, a very successful physician, felt that his son should follow in his footsteps. He couldn't understand why his son constantly complained and expressed a lack of interest in his subjects. Richard's mother said that her son seemed different from the rest of the family. For years his parents had tried to figure him out.

Sam suggested that Richard take a career guidance test. He also thought it would be good for Richard and his parents to take the Myers-Briggs Personality Type Indicator assessment.

When Richard and his parents came back to the office to receive their reports from the MBTI, Sam gave a brief explanation about personality types and what their reports might mean. He asked the three family members to read their own reports, then swap reports and read each other's.

When they returned the following week, all of them commented on how helpful the information had been. For the first time, they were beginning to understand each other's differences. Mom and dad smiled and said, "This has finally helped us figure out Richard." Richard also smiled as he confessed that for years he couldn't understand what was wrong with his parents. Now he could see that many of those "wrongs" were just differences.

Richard was the only N (Intuitive) of the three. He was very interested in possibilities and seeing things as they could be. He had a variety of interests: mountain-climbing, concerts, wilderness camps, hiking, canoeing and snow skiing.

His parents, S (Sensing) types, were very realistic and factual. They had fewer interests and they described their interests as more "traditional." They enjoyed traveling to large cities and attending theater, the symphony and museums. They valued greatly meaningful family gatherings, which unfortunately bored Richard.

Richard's mother, the only F (Feeling) type in the group, was concerned about how her family and friends viewed her son's poor performance in school.

Richard and his dad, on the other hand, weren't that concerned about the opinions of their family and friends. After all, facts were facts: they both openly admitted that Richard was barely passing his courses at the university.

Richard's father, the only I (Introvert) in the group, seldom initiated social activities with their friends. By contrast, Richard and his mother always needed and sought out a lot of social contact. They wondered why Richard's father seemed to be so quiet. Yet when he spoke, you could count on his insights being well thought out. Richard's dad was amazed at the risks Richard and his mother were willing to take.

As Sam continued to work with the family, it was obvious how much they gained from understanding themselves. Their acceptance of themselves and each other improved markedly.

Richard's personality type report also revealed some helpful career guidance information. It listed several vocations which attracted a high percentage of people with a personality type like his. When this information was combined with a career guidance assessment, a couple of common denominators surfaced. One of the common denominators was environmental science.

With this information and Richard's interest, his dad's insistence that his son follow in his footsteps began to fade. Sam suggested some of the career opportunities that were available in environmental science. He drew their attention to a newspaper article that described the increased demand for people trained in this field. Richard's parents began to change their outlook.

Richard found several school catalogues with strong departments in environmental science, and he decided to change schools. The second quarter Richard made the Dean's list; two years later he graduated with honors. After graduating, he had several good job offers and was also considering going on to graduate school. Richard's parents were very proud of him!

Improving Communication

The example of Richard and his parents shows how understanding themselves and each other led to a greater degree of acceptance in their family. Communication was also enhanced between them. The second benefit of understanding and appreciating different personality types is: improving interpersonal communication.

In this book, we are primarily concerned with you and your child. One of the common complaints in parent-child relationships is difficulty in communicating or lack of communication. Our favorite definition of communication:

Communication is not what is said, but what is heard.

At the heart of our personality type is taking in information and making decisions with that information. If you and your child differ in one or two letters in these areas, then it is easy to see how communication could be difficult. At issue here is understanding and accepting that words that you value and make sense to you may not be words that your child values or make sense to them.

For example, if you are an S (Sensing) person and your child is an N (Intuitive) — or vice versa — then you may both perceive what is said differently. A Sensing person chooses words dealing with facts. When an Intuitive person hears these words, he immediately begins to use his imagination and to see possibilities. A Sensing parent might look at an Intuitive child and think he's out in the "O Zone" somewhere!

Or suppose you both have the same preferences for perception, but you don't make decisions in the same way. You may organize and structure information differently which could also lead to misunderstanding.

Instead of trying to change your child and bring him in from his "Zone," appreciate and encourage his natural capability. In training up your child in the way he should go, instruction and teaching are critical to that training. Again, personality differences could make this difficult. If you understand and accept how your child organizes and processes what you say, then your teaching will be much more effective.

Most children are apt to listen more effectively to those adults who accept their differences. The conflict is less, tension released, the air cleared and a pleasant exchange of information can take place.

Someone once said: "If a child doesn't learn the way you teach, then teach the way he learns."

Also be sure to compliment or reward your child in a way that is meaningful to him. If there is a difference in personality type, what you appreciate may be unappreciated and have little value to your child.

How can we keep differences from damaging our interpersonal relationships, especially with our children?

First, we must clearly recognize the damaging effects of selfishness (demanding others to do it our way). We cannot eliminate selfishness from our lives but we can ask the Lord to control it as we become more submissive to Him and learn to walk in the Spirit.

As you ask the Lord to control your selfishness and use your understanding of personality differences, you will begin to see improvements in family relationships.

You'll need patience as you start to use these insights in dealing with your family relationships. Wrong thinking and habits may have dominated your life for a long time. However, the Lord will guide and strengthen you as you form new habits and ways of thinking. Because of His help, it will take less time to form new positive habits.

Looking at those you love in this new light, see how many differences have been mislabeled as wrongs in your family. Carefully and honestly reevaluate your list of wrongs. Understanding the above information should help you do this. Obviously some of the wrongs are wrongs or character flaws. These need time and patience to correct.

We have been amazed by how many times this approach has solved many difficult marriage and parent-child relationships.

For many years as counselors, we felt that many "bad" relationships had been improved to "good". But once we began using the MBTI assessment and we saw people use the information learned from it, the "good" was even more improved to "better."

We don't want to imply that because you understand personality differences, you have to settle back, "bite the bullet" and continue to cope with these "different" people. There's a better way!

Use these differences constructively. Encourage your children in the areas of their personality preferences. There will be chores or jobs around the house that each of them can do better and easier than you or a brother or sister.

If selfishness isn't viewed and treated as sin and then controlled by the Holy Spirit, these differences can again become destructive. So always keep a watchful eye out for the subtle natural influence of selfishness.

When we first learned about personality differences, we were fascinated by the insights we gained into our own and others' behavior. Our interest has continued to grow.

Sam was convicted about how he had mislabeled our children wrong when they were different. He was blind to the effects of selfishness in his relationships with our children.

Sam's fourth letter in his personality type is J. Our son Mark's fourth letter is a P. Both fit the mold very well in this area of their personality type. To refresh your memory, the J represents a work-play-work person and the P represents a play-work-play person. Mark can easily leave the grass uncut and enjoy his golf game. It bothers Sam to leave work undone. Both may have plans to cut the grass; it is simply a matter of when they choose to do the work. This explains why Sam had placed the wrong label on Mark that one strained Saturday morning.

Rookie of the Year!

Today Mark is a very successful commercial real estate agent. He began his real estate career in residential sales. Much of this kind of work is done on the weekends. However, during the summer and deer season Mark spent many weekends on the golf course or in the woods.

One Friday at noon, Sam called Mark at work. The receptionist said Mark wasn't in the office. He asked when Mark would be back. She said he was gone for the day. Sam asked if she knew where Mark had gone. "He's gone to play golf," she said.

Sam shook his head. "Friday noon, on the golf course," he sighed. "Nothing has changed. Will he ever be able to succeed?"

One year later Mark had sold over one million dollars of real estate and was nominated as, "Rookie of the Year." That afternoon on the golf course he had launched the largest deal he has ever made! Guess who was pleasantly surprised, while at the same time puzzled?

Mark has used his "different" personality type to great advantage.

Unfortunately, we didn't learn about personality type and the Myers-Briggs Type Indicator assessment until after Mark had left our home and was well into his career. As Sam reflected on these incidents with Mark after learning about personality type, he cried and laughed. He cried because he realized how much his selfishness had damaged his relationship with his son. At the same time, he couldn't help laughing at the accuracy and truth of the personality type descriptions. As we read and learned from these descriptions, it seemed that someone had come to live in our house and had written down what they observed!

Continuing in the Way He Should Go

Let's examine the latter part of our opening proverb: "... and when he is old he will not depart from it" (Proverbs 22:6b). If you factor in personality type in communicating with your child as you train him, there is a greater possibility that he will hear you. If he hears you, then it is likely that he will understand you. As you faithfully help him obey, your child will be forming good habits at an early age. Remember, habits are first cobwebs, then cables. As you see that your child obeys, you are helping him build a strong, multi-stranded cable. This cable will help him "continue in the way that he should go." It takes years to build a strong cable, so be patient and hang in there! It'll be worth it!

In this chapter we've given you only a minimum amount of information about personality type. We hope that we've whetted your appetite and you'll want to learn more. The more we've used the information gained from the Myers-Briggs Type Indicator assessment, the more excited we've become. Seek out a local counselor or psychologist who is qualified to administer the MBTI assessment.

After you've taken the assessment, which only takes about thirty-five minutes, your choices will give you an accurate picture of your personality type. Then you may enjoy reading one of several excellent books that describe each of the sixteen personality types. We've included a list of recommended books at the end of this book.

The information is practical and easy to apply. And how rewarding it will be to have a deeper understanding of yourself and your child. In managing children you are working toward behavior change. They also need a changed heart and spirit. Be sure you know the difference between personality difference and rebelliousness.

It is very important to remember that you and/or your child's personality type is not an excuse for anything.

In closing, let's return to where we started: "Train up a child in the way he should go (and in keeping with his individual gift or bent)" (Proverbs 22:6a). Understanding your child's personality will help you appreciate how God has uniquely gifted him or her to be. As a wise and sensitive parent, you then can train your child in a way that brings out the best in your son or daughter.

Understanding and appreciation of differences can help equip you to train a child, but even the most conscientious parents still need something more to make these principles work on a daily basis — love. If you have all understanding, says the Bible, but don't have love, you've gained nothing (I Corinthians 13:2).

Love is the main ingredient in God's recipe for family living. We believe that God has given us some unique and practical insights into love. As we've put these insights into practice, they have led to some of the most profound experiences in our Christian lives. Love is the subject of our next chapter. Read on!

FOR
ME

CHAPTER **8**
LOVE: A
QUEST
FOR THE BEST

CHAPTER VIII

Love: A Quest For The Best

"Eagerly pursue and seek to acquire (this) love — make it your aim, your great quest..."

I Corinthians 14:1 (AMP)

Leah had lived at the Good Shepherd Convent in Manila, Philippines for ten years. Her mother wasn't married when she was born and she had never known her father. When Leah was five years old, her mother married a man who hated the sight of her. He told her many times a day to get lost.

The little girl was a bother to the newlyweds as well as a reminder of her mother's past. One day Leah decided to do what she had been told — get lost. She went into the crowded, dirty streets of her neighborhood and wandered among the crowds.

Night comes quickly in Manila. Leah was afraid of the dark. To find comfort she went into one of the large cathedrals and hid herself in the confessional booth.

The priest found her and took her to the convent. Leah liked living in the convent. But by the time she was fifteen, she had to be sent to the hospital about three times a year. For no apparent reason, she would scream and pull her hair out by the handfuls. She was put in a strait jacket on the psychiatric ward of the hospital until she was calm. She couldn't be left alone because of the harm she might do to her own body.

The Mother Superior didn't want to put Leah back in a strait jacket, but she didn't know what else to do. I had been teaching a Bible class for the sisters of the convent. The Mother Superior asked me to come and talk to Leah.

I agreed to talk with her, but as I drove to the convent I felt hesitant. I wasn't trained to help mentally disturbed people. I only knew what the Bible taught about emotions. I could only share what I knew.

I found Leah sitting on a bench under a tree, her hands folded in her lap, her feet crossed under the bench. She looked at the ground, her black, shiny hair hanging down on both sides of her face. All I could see was hair until she looked up at me.

Leah was a beautiful young lady. Big brown eyes, beautiful skin, lovely white teeth. But she never smiled. The expression on her face never changed.

"Hello, Leah," I said softly. "My name is Mrs. Peeples. The Mother Superior asked me to come and talk with you. She said you were having problems and she wanted me to be your friend." Leah nodded and moved over on the bench, making room for me to sit next to her.

I explained that I was a missionary from the United States and I had come to tell people in the Philippines how much God loved them. I told her that God loved her so much that He sent His Son, whose name was Jesus, to live on earth and experience life just as we experience it.

Leah listened attentively. She never moved a muscle as she looked me in the eye. I told her that Jesus lived a perfect life and then died on the cross to forgive us our sins and to give us eternal life. I asked Leah if she had ever invited Jesus Christ to come into her life. She said, "no." I asked if she would like to have Him come into her life and she said, "yes."

We bowed our heads and she prayed with me. After our prayer I told her that when Jesus Christ comes to live in our life the Bible teaches that we become children of God. I had her read John 1:12 in my Bible, "But as many as received him, to them gave he power to become the sons of God, even to them that believe on his name" (KJV).

Our time was up, and I had to leave. Since Leah didn't have a Bible, I asked if I could come the next day and bring her one. I gave her a little booklet to read when she went to bed that night. She was pleased that I was going to visit again. Yes, she assured me, she would appreciate her own Bible.

Finally, a Father

The next day when I drove into the convent grounds, I saw Leah sitting on a post at the entrance. I hardly recognized her. She ran to the car, screaming, "Mrs. Peeples, Mrs. Peeples!"

Leah didn't wait for me to get out of the car. She was talking so fast and so loud, I could hardly keep up with what she was saying.

"Yesterday when you told me God loved me," she said, "that was the first time in my life anyone ever said they loved me. I've never heard those words in my entire life! My mom never wanted me. My stepfather wanted to get rid of me. I've never heard anyone say they loved me."

As Leah talked, I got out of my car and walked with her to "our" bench. Leah continued, "I have lived here for ten years and the sisters have been so good to care for me. I appreciate all they've done, but I want a family. Every night when I go to sleep I've prayed and asked God to give me a father. I want a father so much!"

I was fighting to keep back tears as I listened to Leah. Her face was literally shining and her eyes were like stars. She was smiling and talking as fast as possible. "Oh, Ma'am," she said, "last night I read the verse we read together. As I was saying my prayers, I realized I *have* a Father! The verse says if you receive Jesus Christ, and I did, you become a child of God!"

I couldn't believe what I was hearing. God was revealing the truth to this young girl in an unbelievable manner. She understood the verses I had shared in such a practical way. Leah said over and over, "Ma'am, I have a Father and He will never tell me to go away, and He will never go away from me!"

I met with Leah each week after that and we learned more about her new Father. Imagine my surprise when one Monday morning the Mother Superior called to tell me that Leah was becoming depressed. I had better hurry to the convent. I threw on my clothes and took off!

A Giant in My Life

"What can I tell Leah now?" I wondered. I had told her everything I knew. I asked God to help me help Leah. As we sat together on our bench under the tree, I suddenly decided to read Leah a story about a teenage boy. I had no idea where I was going with the story of David and Goliath, but I wanted to read it to her anyway.

As we finished the story of the giant killing, Leah put her hand on my arm and said, "Ma'am, I have a giant in my life. It's my mother. Please go tell my mother about Jesus Christ so she can invite Him into her life."

I knew it didn't work that way! You can't just go tell someone about God and have them pray as Leah had done. I asked where her mother lived. Frankly, I was surprised that she knew. I found out that the sisters in the convent had located her and kept in touch, but Leah's mother had made no attempt to have any contact with her daughter.

This was Leah's giant. She wanted her mother to love her, and she believed God could work a miracle in her mother's life. Leah told me that her mother lived on an island five hundred miles from Manila.

When she said this, I felt relieved. I told Leah I couldn't possibly go to this island because it was too far away. With absolutely no hesitation, Leah said she would pray that I would be able to go.

You probably have guessed that Sam came home in four weeks and told me we had been invited to conduct a conference on this island! I went to the convent and told Leah that God had answered her prayers.

Terrified

When we arrived at the conference at the Good Shepherd Convent on the island of Cebu in Cebu City, I asked one of the sisters to help me find Leah's mother. She knew immediately where she was: Leah's mother was a famous movie star! I asked if she would take me to see her. She was shocked that I wanted to go, but was willing.

The nun and I climbed into the back seat of a jeep, and our driver took us to see Leah's mother. I was terrified when I knocked on that door. I prayed that she wouldn't be home. Suddenly, a beautiful woman opened the door. Not knowing what to say, I blurted out, "I'm a friend of your daughter's, and she asked me to come tell you what I told her!" I was invited to come inside.

We sat on the sofa, and I told Leah's mother the same story I told Leah. I asked her the same question: had she ever invited Jesus Christ to come into her life? She gave me the same answer Leah had given me. She bowed her head and prayed to invite Jesus Christ to come into her life. We read the verse in John and I explained what happens when Christ comes into a person's life.

Frankly, I left as soon as possible. I wasn't sure about this visit. Filipinos are very gracious and kind. I wondered if she was sincere with her prayer or if she was just being courteous to me.

As soon as I returned to Manila, I went to the convent and told Leah what had happened. I felt I had to be honest and prepare her for disappointment. "Leah, don't get your hopes up," I said. "It might take your mother a long time to change. She might *not* change, and I don't want you to get depressed again." She assured me that she was fine and that she would pray for her mother.

Three weeks later I got a telephone call from the convent. Leah was leaving the convent. I asked where she was going. The woman from

the convent said she didn't know, but she knew I had spent time with
Leah and she thought I would want to know that she would no longer
be living there.

I was shocked. My heart felt strange, as if I had lost something precious. I had. Where did Leah go? And why didn't she call me?

Just then our doorbell rang. When I went to the door, I saw Leah
and her mother standing arm in arm. They ran into my living room
and both began to cry. Leah's mom gave me a hug and said, "Mrs.
Peeples, I didn't think too much about that prayer we prayed, but several days later something happened inside me. God began to put a
love in my heart for Leah that I've never had. This love increased and
increased until I felt I couldn't stand it. I had to come for her. My husband saw my anguish, and agreed for me to come and get her. First I
am taking Leah to vacation in the mountains. We need to get to know
each other. Then on to Cebu. She is coming home to her family. Her
family who loves her!"

Without Love, You Can Go Crazy

Leah put her arms around me and said, "Thank you, Ma'am, for
telling me about Jesus, and for telling my mother about Him. Thank
you for making me understand how God can be my heavenly Father
and now He has given me an earthly family!" Leah and her mother
left arm in arm like two lovers. Leah did go to live in Cebu where she
finished high school and went to college. The last time I heard from
Leah she was making TV commercials. The last time I saw her, she
had a white towel tied around her head. Her eyes shone like bright

stars and her beautiful teeth sparkled as she looked into the camera and told the audience about the wonderful bar of soap she held in her hand.

Leah taught me a great lesson. She taught me that without love, you can go crazy. For many years, Leah had lived in a comfortable dormitory and wore nice uniforms provided by the convent. The food was good, the facilities great, the education excellent, but it wasn't enough. Nothing matters if nobody loves you. All the comforts this world offers and all the opportunities you have don't take the place of a mother or a father's love. Just knowing someone cares and is there for you is what children need to make the rest of life fit into place.

Leah could deal with the loneliness for a while, but finally the need for love would overwhelm her; she would literally scream and pull her hair out by the roots. She went temporarily insane because of her great and uncontrollable need to be loved.

Leah's mother taught me another lesson. God is able! He is completely able and willing to change a heart. God *is* love; therefore, He is the source of all love.

The Greatest Need

Everyone needs to love someone and be loved by someone — especially children. Nothing is more needed in parenting than for parents to love their children. And how husbands and wives need to love each other! Someone, while speaking about the husband's responsibility in the home, said, "The greatest thing a father can do for a child is to love his mother." The same should is true of moms loving dads.

Unger's Bible Dictionary summarizes why love should be our top priority: "Love is the highest motive or ground of moral actions. Without this, all other motives fall short of furnishing the true stimulus of Christian living. As all sin roots itself in selfishness, so all virtue springs out of love."

It was love that motivated God to provide for our salvation. "For God so loved the world, that he gave his only begotten Son, that whosoever believeth in him should not perish, but have everlasting life" John 3:16 (KJV).

Love is the true test of discipleship, and thus was the major emphasis of the first century church. Jesus said, "By this shall all men know that ye are my disciples, if ye have love one to another" John 13:35 (KJV). During the intervening years, this emphasis was lost. Love didn't characterize much of the reformation, and churches today are the products of the reformation. We need to recapture the spirit of discipleship of the first century church — the spirit of love. Love is often misunderstood. How would you define it? Where would you turn for a definition? For many, TV and its soap operas provide a ready source. Or what about the latest romance novel or magazine? What about the Bible? If you look in the Bible, you will find a much greater emphasis given to what love *is*, than to what it *does*. When we hear the word, love, we automatically assume it refers to something we do. It's difficult to think of love as an "is" word.

More than a Four Letter Word

Let's look at how love is described in the Bible in I Corinthians 13:4-8a. I Corinthians 13 is often referred to as the "love chapter" in the Bible; it certainly reveals the most complete picture of what love is. In most translations as you begin reading in verse four, the second word is, "is." Notice it doesn't say what love does, it simply says love is!

Following the word "is," there is a list of love's twenty characteristics. Love is more than a four letter word! In the list are words that describe two kinds of spiritual/emotional traits - those that we need in our lives and those that love protects us from.

We looked in a number of translations for words in the list that best communicated to us. The list below is a mixture taken from the *King James Version* and *The Living Bible*:

1. suffers long and is kind
2. never jealous
3. never envious
4. never boastful
5. never proud
6. never haughty
7. never selfish
8. never rude
9. does not demand its own way
10. not irritable
11. not touchy
12. does not hold grudges
13. hardly even notices when others do it wrong
14. never glad about an injustice
15. rejoices whenever truth wins out
16. bears all things
17. believes all things
18. hopes all things
19. endures all things
20. never fails

When you ask God to make you a loving person, these are the things you can expect to occur or not to occur in your life. Love is the only fruit of the Spirit that is so multi-faceted. Where can you find such qualities as peace or joy followed by a twenty-word list of characteristics?

Reread the list carefully. As you do, you'll realize as we have, that it "covers the waterfront."

All that we need to be or not be is found in the list. Can you see why love is the key word in the Bible? It's at the heart of the greatest commandment of them all, "Master, which is the great commandment in the law? Jesus said unto him, Thou shalt love the Lord thy God with all thy heart, and with all thy soul, and with all thy mind. This is the first and great commandment. And the second is like unto it, Thou shalt love thy neighbour as thyself. On these two commandments hang all the law and the prophets." Matthew 22:36-40 (KJV).

Jesus also said love is the test of discipleship. As a Christian parent, you need to be sure you're a disciple of Jesus. As a disciple, love for your child will be a high priority.

Notice that love is a fruit of the Spirit, not the fruit of a good marriage or having an obedient child. Letting the Holy Spirit control your life allows God to make you a loving person. The kind of love that produces a harmonious relationship between you and your child is not generated from within the parent-child relationship. It is from God and depends on your walking in fellowship with Him.

In premarital counseling, we tell couples that it is better to marry a loving person, than a person in love!

Taking Your "Love Pulse"

How do you know if you're a loving person? For the first twenty years of our Christian lives, we thought it was measured by the response we received as we loved others. This can be very discouraging. Love guarantees nothing in return from those whom we've made objects of our love! What then does it guarantee? Love guarantees that its twenty characteristics will be more and more a part of your life!

You can take your "love pulse" at any time during the day. Just review the list and see how you're doing. You will never get a perfect grade, but your grade should improve. There will always be a few characteristics that need more attention than others.

God's love for us is unconditional; ours should be the same for our children. We can choose to be a loving parent, but we have no control over our children's response. When you realize love guarantees nothing in return, it protects you from being disappointed by your children's behavior.

The parent-child relationship reveals our need to be loving like no other relationship. But don't make the mistake of looking to your children as the source of love.

We are told in I Thessalonians 3:12, "And the Lord make you to increase and abound in love one toward another, and toward all men, even as we do toward you:(KJV). Love should be ongoing in our lives. The word "increase" refers to the quality of our love and the word "abound" refers to the quantity of our love.

If you ask God to cause your love to increase and abound, the above list describes what will happen in your life. You will be free to make love your greatest aim when you realize this list is not dependent on circumstances or on other people.

Becoming a Loving Person

Rebecca was struggling with a rebellious teenage daughter and a husband whose career kept him on the road. Sam had spent months with her in counseling. As a committed Christian, Rebecca was disappointed in her constant reactions of anger and resentment. Sam explained what we've told you about love. She seemed to understand, but had difficulty applying it to her situation. She had been praying so much for her daughter and couldn't understand why she didn't see changes.

A few days after one of Rebecca's visits, she called the office and expressed her excitement over what the Lord had shown her. Instead of praying to become a loving person herself, she had been praying for her daughter to become lovable!

Rebecca realized that she had been praying for the daughter to change so she could love her. She needed to love her daughter when she was lovable, and when she wasn't lovable. Rebecca continued to pray for her daughter to change, but she began to spend more time praying for her own love to increase and abound toward her daughter. It was soon apparent that love was working in Rebecca's life because her bouts of anger and resentment occurred less frequently.

Rebecca pointed out some very practical ways she knew that love was beginning to take hold in her life. "I'm not as irritable or touchy," she reflected. "I hardly notice when my daughter does me wrong. I don't bear a grudge against her, and I'm becoming more kind as I go through the long-suffering of raising a rebellious teenager." Rebecca was going through an heir-raising experience!

What would it take for your love to increase and abound? Would your child have to change? Or does this verse tell you that your love increasing and abounding has nothing to do with your child, but has everything to do with you and the Lord.

It is much easier to do loving things than to be a loving person. You don't have to be a Christian to do loving things. However, to become a loving person requires change, and we all resist change. Are you willing to let the Lord change you so you can be a loving parent?

Love is concerned first with what we are, but love also takes action. What is the greatest thing you can do for your children? The greatest thing you can do for your child is to be a loving parent. Can you imagine what it would be like for your child to have a parent whose life was characterized by love more and more.

What Love Did for One Boy

Carl, a prominent business, civic and church leader in our city told us a story about his family. As he shared the story, he didn't seem to think it was very important. Little did he know that what he was telling us would have a profound impact on our family.

When Carl was a little boy, living in a small rural community in Alabama, his mother and father separated. Carl is now a grandfather, and until this day he hasn't heard from or seen his father.

His grandparents took his mother and the four children in and cared for them. Carl told us that his grandparents and his aunts were thrilled to have his mother and her children. Carl laughed as he said that he had so much love from his grandmother, grandfather and aunts, he didn't know he was from a dysfunctional family until he started hearing about dysfunctional families!

He said he grew up with two pairs of overalls and a lot of love, a happy, well-adjusted boy. Carl now has a lovely wife and three outstanding children.

We listened to Carl's story with great interest. Our daughter was going through a divorce and was about to move home with Sam and me. One of our major concerns was how the divorce would effect our two grandsons.

Sam and I left church after talking with Carl with new hope. We love our daughter and our grandchildren. We were fortunate enough to have a house that could accommodate us all. We have access to the Source of Love. Our grandsons can one day say to someone what Carl said to us. How great it will be to hear those little guys say, "Our grandparents loved us so much, we had a great time living with them and we never knew we were from a broken home!"

Such examples offer hope in seemingly hopeless situations. If we listened to what the media says about all the problems facing children of divorce, we would definitely have a sense of hopelessness. The media seems to imply that all broken homes are dysfunctional. Carl's story was certainly an exception! Perhaps media-makers aren't familiar with the power of God's love.

Sam and I are confident that our grandsons, Mark and Gil, will look back with delight over those days they lived in our home with us. We are four years away from that time and even now they mention the fun we had playing in the rain, having a picnic in the back yard, raking leaves together and enjoying big Sunday dinners after church.

Today our daughter has her own house and supports her children. We still have picnics together and sometimes we even sit down to a big Sunday dinner at our house. The fun continues with her family because of the relationships we've established. Without love in our hearts, that year would have been a total disaster. Instead of drawing us closer, lack of love could have driven a wedge between us.

Yes, love is an "is" word, but love takes action too. Love isn't selfish or self-centered. Love shares with a grateful heart. How do you know you're a loving person? When an opportunity comes to help others, you take advantage of the opportunity and enjoy doing it.

Is Love Passive?

Very often we are misunderstood by emphasizing the need to *be* a loving person. Some people feel we are promoting a passive Christian lifestyle. Nothing could be further from the truth! If you love someone, you want the best for them.

Love does not accept bad behavior, because it desires the best for others.

If your child is doing something wrong, you should put a stop to it because you desire the best for them. Accepting their wrong behavior is not good for them! There are three reasons for taking action:

1. For God's sake. Their behavior is not pleasing to God. Christian parents should desire that their children's behavior be in line with God's standard, the Bible.
2. For your children's sake. How can they have a good self-image if you allow them to refuse your instruction?
3. For the relationship's sake. You can't have a good relationship with your child if you tolerate wrong behavior.

Burned Up!

Several years ago, a missionary friend came home from the field, and spent some time with us. She had been on the mission field for thirty-five years, returning home every four years for deputation work.

Edie said her heart felt burdened by what she saw happening in the church in America. Do you remember the story of the frog who was put in cold water? The temperature was gradually increased until the water was boiling. The frog died and never knew what happened. Many Christians today have third degree burns and they're aren't sure how it happened! In counseling, it is not uncommon to hear Christians say, "I'm burned up!"

Historians might one day write about the church in America wondering why it was so large and never turned the country upside down! In Acts 17:6, many of the first century Christians were referred to as, "These that have turned the world upside down."

As Edie came home every four years she saw love growing cold in the church. Why doesn't love prevail? Matthew speaks to this very clearly, "And because iniquity shall abound, the love of many shall wax cold" Matthew 24:12 (KJV). "Iniquity" means selfishness!

Another friend said, "It might be good for us not to have bread and need to ask our neighbor for a slice." It's easy to give, but hard to receive. Unless we learn to receive love from God, how can we share it with others? You can't give away what you don't have.

No one wants to suffer and that includes us. However, we all know that often during a time of crisis, people work together, help and share in a loving way. What a shame that it sometimes takes a crisis for us to realize how much we need to depend on God to be our source of love.

What a difference it would make in our country if we were all motivated by love in the causes we stand for and in the tasks we strive to accomplish.

It Only Takes a Spark

History teaches that when the family begins to break down, the nation soon decays. Is the task of stopping decay in our nation insurmountable? You may be concerned as we are, but wonder, what can one person do? Can one voice really make a difference? It's true that you are only one, but you can be the one to make a difference in your family. Our prayer is that many concerned men and women will join you in curbing the decay in our land. It only takes a spark to get a fire going!

It takes a spark to get a fire going, but it takes real dedication to keep the fire burning. Parents need to renew their dedication from time to time. Raising children can be time consuming, frustrating and expensive. There are days when you're ready to give up, throw in the towel and walk away. These are the days we suggest you take a good long look at your child and ask yourself, "Is he/she worth the effort?" We hope you'll answer, "yes"!

Now is the time to renew your dedication, ". . . lift up the hands which hang down, and the feeble knees; And make straight paths for your feet, lest that which is lame be turned out of the way; but let it rather be healed" Hebrews 12:12,13 (KJV).

Let's join hands, understanding what is involved in making a commitment to our families, and let's make a difference in our world! We can turn it upside down or should we say right side up!

CHAPTER 9

MAKING A
COMMITMENT

CHAPTER IX

Making A Commitment

"Commit thy way unto the Lord; trust also in Him; and He shall bring it to pass."

Psalm 37:5 (KJV)

In 1975, we were asked to consider moving from the Philippines to Spain to work in a lay ministry with people in local churches. Sam told the director of our mission that his first consideration would have to be to our children. His commitment was to God first, his family second and his ministry third.

Our eldest son, Sam, had graduated from high school and was off to college in the United States. Dawn had two years left in high school and Mark had three years left.

Dawn had made many friends in the Philippines. She knew that she could make friends wherever she lived. Her life was exciting as long as she had a friend, and it was even more exciting if she had a friend plus a boyfriend. We wanted her to have the opportunity to go to a school with a good scholastic reputation. We also wanted a school where she could develop socially. Athletics had become an important part of Mark's life. He had been on the starting team in basketball, volleyball and soccer. Every afternoon his time was spent practicing some sport. God had gifted Mark with athletic ability; he was a natural athlete.

Sam wanted Mark to attend a school with a strong athletic program, as well as a good scholastic reputation. We packed our possessions, left them with a broker at the dock in Manila and went to check out the school situation in Spain.

Our son, Sam, and daughter, Dawn, went to the United States to stay with friends. Mark went with us to Spain. The man who met us at the airport asked what our agenda was for our stay in his country. Sam said the first stop should be the high school. We knew if the school was not acceptable, any other investigation would be a waste of time.

Mark, fourteen at the time, was wondering if his dad really intended to make a decision about where we lived based on the school. He heard what his dad said, but he was waiting to see if he would do what he said!

We went to the American School, a school for children of missionaries and of American businessmen. We parked in front of a large home that had been converted into the school. Beside the school was a large, open, grassy field. On the edge of the field near the school stood a large oak tree. As we walked toward the door, I noticed a basketball backboard attached to the tree. The rim didn't have a net. Sam looked at Mark. Mark's expression was a mixture of shock, surprise and disappointment. Sam turned to Mark and said, "We're tourists!"

Mark breathed a sigh of relief and a smile appeared on his face. Dad really did mean what he said!

Sam had already decided that Mark's school and his opportunity to further develop his athletic ability took precedent over where we would minister. Of course we prayed about where the Lord would have us serve. And we believe God gave us these convictions about Dawn, Mark and the school. These convictions provided a tangible means of helping determine the Lord's will.

The next few years would be very important for our children. They needed a father who would keep his priorities in order. The Lord could raise up someone to work in that city. He didn't need someone to fill that job who was knowingly out of His will because he didn't honor his convictions regarding his children.

Keep Your Priorities in Order

We see two things lacking in many families that concern us: discipline and commitment. If parents are not disciplined and committed, then it is hard to instill these traits in their children. We've discussed discipline in a previous chapter, now let's look at commitment.

Webster defines *commitment* as "the act of pledging or entrusting." When a man and woman repeat Christian wedding vows, they are making pledges to God and to each other, "before God and these witnesses." In examining what the Bible and the wedding vows say about marriage, it is clear that the key to marriage is commitment! The same commitment is required in parenting.

"Man carries his beliefs, but commitment carries the man," as a friend of ours, John Williamson, puts it.

We are to honor the commitments we make. They should not be taken lightly. We need to stick to them! "Observe the postage stamp," we read in a magazine recently, "its usefulness depends upon its ability to stick to one thing until it gets there."

What are the things you should stick to? How do you prioritize your commitments? In Ephesians 5:17-6:9, you will see the following priorities given in the chronological order of these verses:

1. God
2. Spouse
3. Children
4. Work

Marriage was God's idea, not man's. Since our Creator established marriage and the family as the first institution, it seems logical that He would provide instructions to help us carry out our responsibilities.

Problems arise when husbands and wives are not familiar with God's instructions, or when they are familiar with them, but there is no ongoing commitment to carry them out. Review these priorities again and again.

For moms, the most common mistake is to let children move to number two, taking priority over husbands — even becoming their first priority! For dads, it is allowing number four, work, to become number two on the priority list, even number one!

It becomes even more important to keep the proper priorities when parents remarry. Especially when each (or even one) bring children into the home. In these situations you have his, hers and then later possibly ours. The opportunity to get your priorities out of order is much greater. This will place a strain on the marriage.

Be careful not to let this happen. Believe it or not, one day you will end up as you started, just the two of you. The term, "empty nest syndrome," was coined because of problems that arise when children leave home. Husbands and wives need to be sure that they remain friends through these parenting years. This is difficult at times, but it will be worth it. In a sense, your parenting responsibilities never end; they just take on different forms. We thought that our children would grow up, marry and leave home (and they did), but then they multiplied and came back!

Socrates made the following speech in Athens, Greece in 469 B.C., "If I could get to the highest place in Athens, I would lift up my voice and say, 'What mean ye fellow citizens, that you turn every stone to scrape wealth together and take so little care of your children, to whom you must one day relinquish it all?" This question is very appropriate for our day.

Someone once said, "Vision without commitment is fantasy. Commitment without vision is drudgery." To prevent parenting from becoming a drudgery, you need to have a clear vision of what you are committed to. If you allow your Creator to give you that vision, through the Bible, then it will be twenty-twenty all the time!

What are we asking you to be committed to? All of the principles that have been described in the previous chapters. However, you should realize that a lot has been said about a few things. It is best to practice a few things well.

Psalms 37:5 clearly states that your first commitment needs to be to the Lord. Then trust the Lord to lead you in the way He would have you go — in your personal life and in your role as a parent. Your second commitment needs to be to your mate.

Let the Children Come to Me

Your next commitment is to your child. When a Christian is asked, "What is the most important thing that has ever happened to you?" the answer should come without delay, "Asking Jesus to come into my life and becoming a Christian."

If this is true, then what is the most important thing you can do for your child? The obvious answer should be to lead them to the Lord. What a wonderful privilege for a parent to be able to share the gospel and encourage their child to make a decision to accept Christ. As a Christian, you are God's heir. Pray and show your heir the way so that she/he can also become God's heir.

"Once when some mothers were bringing their children to Jesus to bless them, the disciples shooed them away, telling them not to bother him. But when Jesus saw what was happening he was very much displeased with his disciples and said to them, "Let the children come to me, for the Kingdom of God belongs to such as they. Don't send them away! I tell you as seriously as I know how that anyone who refuses to come to God as a little child will never be allowed into his Kingdom." Then he took the children into his arms and placed his hands on their heads and he blessed them"

Mark 10:13-16 (TLB).

We are often asked how old a child has to be to make this decision. It is earlier than most parents believe possible.

When Sam and I became Christians, we didn't know how to lead our children to the Lord. Someone recommended a Child Evangelism Bible class. Our children attended one afternoon each week. Sam was six, Dawn five and Mark four. One afternoon after this class each of them said they had invited Jesus into their heart! I'm sure our excitement exceeded theirs. Sam and Dawn loved the class and were eager to take friends. Mark seemed to go because he had no other choice.

When Mark was eleven years old, I had a conversation with him about his behavior. I told him that I was going to change my ways of dealing with him. I apologized for the many times I had lectured him and badgered him about doing what I said. I explained that I loved him and I was going to tell him once to do something. I said, "Mark, I am going to see that you do what I say and God will have to change your heart."

He looked me in the eye and said, "I don't know about God." I reminded him of the Child Evangelism class and he admitted that he "really didn't mean it" when he invited Jesus to come into his life. I asked him if he wanted to ask Jesus into his heart now. He said he wasn't sure. We spent the next hour talking about the person of Jesus Christ. For an eleven-year-old, Mark had some thought provoking questions.

I answered Mark's questions to the best of my ability. I was always afraid that our children would feel pressured to accept the truth of the Bible. I wanted them to accept it with their own free will because of their understanding. I explained the gospel as clearly as possible. I told Mark that I felt God expected me to make it clear to him, but that the decision was his. I believe my job as a mom was to make sure the children knew how to become a Christian.

I asked Mark to repeat to me what he had heard me say. His understanding was perfect. I remember saying, "Now, Mark, I feel good that you know what is involved in becoming a Christian. You can do this when you want to." As I started to walk out of the room, Mark said, "Mom, don't you think I should become a Christian?"

I said, "I sure do!"

He asked me to come back and pray with him. We prayed together and Mark thanked the Lord for sending His Son to die for him. He asked Jesus Christ to come into his life, to forgive his sins and to be his Savior.

Both Sam and Dawn have no doubt that they became Christians at ages six and five. Mark remembers very clearly his decision for Christ when he was eleven.

To Assist You

There are some excellent materials available to assist you in leading your child to Christ:

- *The Four Spiritual Laws,* an excellent little booklet, put out by Campus Crusade for Christ. You may be familiar with the adult version, but there is also a children's version.
- *The Wordless Book,* developed by Child Evangelism, is a simple booklet of colored pages. Each colored page represents a step in the plan of salvation. Easy for children to use and share with a friend.
- Children's Bibles. Most of these have a section in the back of the book with a clear and simple presentation of the plan of salvation.

The plan of salvation can be presented very easily to children. You can, without pressure, encourage them to pray and trust Christ as their Savior and invite Him into their lives. We urge you to be committed to making clear to your children how they can become a Christian.

Sometimes a commitment is made once, but needs to be renewed several times. True contentment comes not from the pursuit of happiness, but from honoring our commitments. Commit yourself to implementing these principles as early as possible in your child's life. To implement something it is best to plan ahead. Remember Noah didn't build the ark in the rain!

If you remain committed to your role as a parent and take the necessary time to supervise, advise, instruct and enjoy your children, you will feel good about your job when the roles change!

CHAPTER 10

WELCOME
to the
HARD
CRUEL
WORLD...
ENTER
HERE

FEELING
GOOD WHEN
THE ROLES CHANGE

CHAPTER X

Feeling Good When The Roles Change

"My son, Never forget the things I've taught you. If you want a long
and satisfying life, closely follow my instructions. Never forget to be
truthful and kind. Hold these virtues tightly. Write them deep within
your heart."

Proverbs 3:1-3

The Plastic Years

They pass so quickly, the days of youth,
And the children change so fast,
And soon they harden in the mold,
And the plastic years are past.

Then shape their lives while they are young,
This be our prayer, our aim,
That each child we raise shall bear
The imprint of HIS name.

Author Unknown

Our first baby was due in two weeks. I remember waking in the
morning and putting my hand on my stomach to feel the little foot
that kept kicking me in the ribs. I could hardly wait for the first labor
pain to strike. Then soon I would hold that little foot in my hand and
look into the face of our first-born child.

One Friday morning at 6:00 that long awaited pain awakened me
from a deep sleep. Sam jumped out of bed and tried to find the car
(which was just outside the kitchen door)! Once we got in the car, Sam
had trouble slipping the gear into reverse. After we did get going, he
ran over the sidewalk as he backed out of the driveway.

I have always regretted that we didn't have a movie camera. We could have made a lot of money producing a comedy for television. I always think of *I Love Lucy* when the events of that day in May, 1957 flash back into my mind.

Sam Peeples III was born at 5:00 in the afternoon on May 10, 1957. Sam took his picture when he was twenty-three hours old since he was the first newborn we had ever seen that was really beautiful!

After five days in the hospital, I was home with our baby. Three weeks later I was dragging around the house, unable to get into my clothes, unable to sleep, scared to death that something would happen to that tiny baby and crying at least once a day. I remember wishing I could put Sam back in my tummy for just one good night's sleep.

Sam came into our lives to stay! He is now thirty-six years old. When I look at pregnant girls, I have two strong thoughts. I used to get excited for them. Now I silently think, "They don't know what they're in for!" My second thought is, "When the baby arrives, they'll never realize how quickly the time will come when that baby will someday leave home to begin a life apart from mom and dad!

Shackled

I remember well how trapped a parent can feel caring for this little bundle of joy! I remember well the frustration and interference a child can be. Taking care of a little baby can be boring at times. Mothers look forward to "Mom's Day Out," and then spend the day worrying about the care the baby is receiving while they're "out"! The child soon goes to kindergarten. I could hardly wait for little Sam to go to kindergarten. (Then I would only have two babies to care for!) I came home after taking Sam to kindergarten and called my husband, crying because I missed little Sam so much.

I say this to assure all of you that I understand the frustrations and the anxieties parents go through. I have but one desire for young moms and dads, and that desire is for you to be content in the stage of parenting in which you find yourself. I was not content, and it is one of my great regrets.

Unshackled

Our roles as parents change. Children really do grow up. They no longer race through the house, eat everything in sight, make a mess in every room, keep the telephone tied up for hours, and keep us in the car taking them to their activities.

The house is quiet and empty. The rooms are clean and neat. Food spoils in the refrigerator because Sam and I can't eat it all. I have five telephones and I have access to them any time I want. At times I sit in the den waiting for Sam to come home and tears fill my eyes as I can almost hear little feet running down the hall to find me. Little voices used to call, "Mom, where are you?"

"In the den," I would answer.

"O.K.," came the reply. There were times they never came to the den, they just wanted to know I was there.

You realize that what I'm describing is the empty nest syndrome. Our nest cleared out. I regret that I wanted the children to grow up quickly, but Sam and I do not regret that our children are on their own. We never allowed them to come between us, so we were never dependent on them to keep us together. Sam was first with me and I was first with him. We raised our children together.

When the house suddenly was quiet, we missed the children but loved the fact that we could finish a sentence, drink our own coke without having to share a sip, enjoy a quiet meal, go out to dinner without asking or even considering anyone else. Freedom at last!

Our children live near us and they're in and out of our house constantly. One Sunday morning we were enjoying a cup of coffee in bed, reading the Sunday paper when we heard a loud knock on the back door. "Who could that be at 8:00 on Sunday morning?" we wondered.

When I got to the door (the loud knocking continued), I opened it to find Gil, our nine-year-old grandson. He was hot and sweaty, his face beaming. "Hi, Meemaw, I rode my bike to see you and granddaddy!" What a sight to see! Freckles, red curly hair, big smile, coming to see grandmom and granddad.

"Come in, Gil," I said. "We haven't had breakfast, have you?"
"Yes," Gil said, "but I would like some more."

"Let's have breakfast in bed," I suggested.

The three of us piled up in our king size bed and had toast, juice and milk as Gil told us about the new friends who recently moved down the street. Then he told us about the afternoon before, riding his bike and ramping at school.

Suddenly, Gil looked at the clock on the bedside table. 8:40! He screamed, "Bye, Meemaw. I love you. I gotta hurry home or I'll be late for Sunday School."

In a flash, Gil was gone. The house was quiet again. Sam and I sat in bed watching him jump on his bike and ride away. We looked at each other and said, "What was that all about?"

The responsibility of raising children is not ours any more. Though I regret the days I was discontent, I have great peace about my role as a mom. Sam and I feel good about the job we did! I don't mean that we did it all right all of the time. We made many mistakes. We are committed to the Lord, and He was (and still is) faithful to show us mistakes we make. Our goal was to admit our mistakes to the children. When an apology was necessary, to the best of our knowledge, we made it. When we needed to take steps to correct a wrong, we took those steps.

A Grateful Heart

I'm grateful that God showed me the selfishness and impatience in my heart when the children were four, five and six years old. I had a sweet black lady that worked for me two days a week. One morning after the children left for kindergarten, Gloria looked at me and said, "I am surprised that you like your boys more than you like your little girl!" What a startling thing for her to say. I was totally unaware that I expressed a preference toward my children. I must have really shown it if Gloria was able to notice.

I was a new Christian when Gloria made this observation. I closed myself in my room and cried. I prayed and asked the Lord to show me if this was true.

During the next few weeks I realized what had been happening. My beautiful little girl was beginning to mock me. She did things the way I did them. She walked in the kitchen one day and ordered her brothers out while she fixed the graham crackers and coke. The tone of her voice and the look on her face were mine exactly.

I began to see my faults mimicked by my little girl and I didn't like it. Words can't describe the pain in my heart when I realized what I was doing. I resented her. I was angry with her because of the things I saw in her that were a reflection of me!

I asked the Lord to search my heart and try my thoughts. I asked Him to forgive me for the bad attitude I had toward Dawn and to cause my love to increase and abound for my little girl.

This was just one of my many experiences in getting in shape to be a mom. Dawn is a grown woman with a career and a family. I feel good about our relationship. I feel good about what God did in my heart when she was a little girl.

Gradually, He took the resentment away and replaced it with love. I feel good about the fact that I loved her as she was growing up. I loved her even when her socks ran down in her shoes and she came home with her new dress dirty and torn. I loved her when she refused to wear the bow in her hair and when she wanted to wear the dress with the lace. I loved her even if she didn't like to play with dolls, but wanted to climb trees and play ball with her brothers.

So often we fail to realize that we can be eaten up with guilt because of our attitudes. We can be good parents on the outside and terrible parents on the inside. It takes God to search a heart and reveal the truth about our motives. Once the job of raising children is over, there is no going back. We need to be in shape for the job and make good use of the days we have to raise them.

Once we have taken care of our heart, there is a great need to understand our child's needs. Mark's first grade teacher called me at mid-term to tell me that he wasn't going to pass to the second grade. He refused to do his work. I was horrified! My child was going to fail first grade! What would my friends say?

My Baby!

I took Mark for psychological testing to find out if he had a learning problem. The doctor called me in to report his findings. He informed me that Mark felt he could do nothing right. I was constantly telling him to stop, come home, don't do that, etc. The doctor told me that Mark believed he was responsible for all the turmoil in our house. He is a loving, caring child and his fear of failure had overwhelmed him.

In his six-year-old mind, he devised a plan to solve his problem. If he didn't try to succeed in school, he wouldn't run the risk of failure. Failure caused an emotional trauma for Mark. This was his way of trying to avoid it. His way was not sensible, but it was the way he had worked out in his mind.

Driving home from the doctor's office, I knew this finding was true. Mark was the child with no fear! He climbed a fifty-foot television tower when he was eighteen months old. The pediatrician said it couldn't be done, but Mark did it.

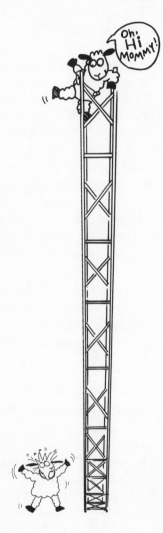

I still remember that harrowing day. I was washing dishes at my mom's house. My dad had just died, and I was spending time with her. As I washed the dishes, I kept calling Mark's name. He would hear me and make a noise. He was outside playing with his bother and sister. After I finished the dishes, I went out to get Mark for his morning bath. I heard him, but couldn't see him. Finally, I looked up and there was my baby, twenty feet off the ground, climbing the tower my dad had erected. I gasped for breath, kept quiet and started climbing the tower to bring him down.

When Mark saw me coming up, he started to laugh and climb higher. I decided to climb down, thinking maybe he would do the same. But he just kept going. I panicked and ran out into the street.

I looked back. There was my little baby wearing only a diaper fifty feet in the air, the height of a five-story building! I stood in the street with my face buried in my hands and cried. A man was working in the yard next door to mom's house. He heard me cry and ran to help. He said, "Lady, what's the matter?"

I answered, "My baby."

He said, "Where is your baby?"

I pointed to the tower and said, "Up there!"

He looked at Mark, and then looked back at me. He said, "Lord God, Jesus," and took off up the tower. He grabbed Mark in his arms and brought him to me. I remember the feeling I had as I held Mark close to my chest. I knew that day that Mark came close to falling to his death, and I felt I couldn't bear the pain of loosing my baby.

That was always the way Mark was. He could climb a brick wall just like a monkey. He climbed trees in a storm to enjoy riding the wind.

My fear of losing him overroad anything else. But I never realized that I was constantly saying no to him. The psychologist was correct in his evaluation of Mark. I could understand Mark's interpretation of my behavior.

I knew Mark needed to be disciplined and supervised, but he also needed encouragement. I understood the problem Mark faced, and fortunately I was in a position to help him.

God could change me and I could understand Mark. Together we could accomplish great changes in both of our lives. I began to pay attention to what I said, the tone of my voice and especially to listen to my voice through his ears.

I feel good about my relationship with Mark. I'm sorry I didn't realize how I constantly "put him down" until he was in the first grade. I didn't intend to do that, but because of his disposition, I had stayed on his "case" too much.

The Basic Three

As you trust God to work in your heart and take the necessary time to understand your child, there are three basic principles apply to most situations:

1. Discipline and punishment are not the same. Discipline is seeing that your child obeys. We recommend you tell your child what to do once, then get up and see that he does it. Punishment is pain, emotional or physical, applied for deliberate disobedience.
2. Be careful when you offer your child an option. Be sure all options are acceptable.
3. Apply light punishment and increase it as slowly as you can. Severe punishment will push your child away and if you increase it too fast, you leave yourself no place to go.

I visited one of my young friends who had just given birth to her second child. Her two-year-old played around her feet as she fed the new baby. I was there for only a few minutes when I realized that the two-year-old was a well adjusted little guy. He was well behaved for a two-year-old who had been receiving all the attention and now had to share it with his competitor.

"You've done a great job with Bradford," I said to Peggy. She laughed and reminded me of a Fourth of July picnic at her mom's house.

Peggy said, "Do you remember sitting around the kitchen table when you told me, 'There are three basic principles you need to remember when you raise a child?' I've never forgotten those three and I've found that one of them always applies to any situation."

"The one that has been the most helpful to me is the one about discipline," she continued. "Tell a child once, get up and make him do what you said." Peggy told me that Bradford assumed that when she was feeding David, she was incapacitated. He was learning that she could and would put David down to come to Bradford when she needed to. He also felt she was incapacitated when she was talking on the telephone, but he was learning that Peggy could interrupt a telephone conversation at any given moment to come to Bradford to make sure that he obeyed. Bradford didn't feel neglected.

I told Peggy's mother about our conversation. She said she remembered one time when she and Peggy had been shopping before David was born. Just as Peggy was making a purchase, Bradford began running through the store. Peggy turned to him and told him to stop. As most two-year-olds would, Bradford kept running. Peggy asked the saleslady to excuse her. She stopped Bradford from running, brought him to stand by her side and finished making her purchase.

Bradford has boundaries and he feels safe. Peggy said it has been easy because she doesn't wait until she is angry and he is frustrated before she gets up and goes to see that he obeys.

The Benefits of Pain

As you raise your children, there will be times when you feel guilty. Guilt causes pain. Pain can be put to good use by God: it is one of the tools He uses to direct our path.

Major Ian Thomas once said that, "Pain is one of man's best friends." Pain in a tooth indicates decay. Pain in the body can indicate cancer. Countless teeth have been saved because of pain. Think of the people who are alive today because of the pain which caused them to seek help from a physician.

Emotional pain can also be a friend. Of course, this is true only when we allow it to motivate us to seek God's help. Just as physical pain is an indicator of physical problems, emotional pain often points to spiritual problems. Emotional pain should drive us to discover the cause. Don't deny emotional pain. Admit it and deal with it. Living with emotional pain can be dangerous. At times our pride can get in the way and keep us from seeking God's help. We are afraid of our peers' derision if they find out we have a problem.

But as William McFee observes, "The world is not interested in the storm you encountered, but did you bring in the ship."

You will go through many storms in raising children. The question is, how do you feel about the job? Regardless of the condition of the ship, you can feel good about the way you brought it through the storms!

Make it your goal to be friends with your adult children and enjoy your grandchildren. Adult children should be on their own and will (or should) leave home. After a visit, they go home and take the grandchildren. It's wonderful to see them come, and good to see them go. Good to see them go when you know they will come back for more fun, fellowship and probably food!

Influence

We are often asked what are the important things to remember when your children grow up and begin families of their own. We believe the most important thing is for parents to be able to influence their children. It is good for an adult child to seek counsel from their parents. We have talked to many young adults who don't want their parents to know anything about their business. What a shame!

We don't mean that parents should control their children's lives. But where harmony and peace exist, conversation can take place. If you have dealt with your heart as a parent and been a loving and kind person, your adult children will know that you have their best interest at heart. Listen to their stories. Give an honest opinion and be willing to accept their decision even if it differs from yours.

We have talked with many parents whose children are marrying mates that these parents dislike. Our advice has been for them to do all they can to reason with their child and try to influence their decision. If they fail in this endeavor, they must maintain a relationship that will protect future avenues of influence.

If your predictions come true about your child's mate and the marriage, your child will need your assistance, counsel and refuge more than ever. If they can't come to you, who will they turn to?

I know how you feel when your children disobey you. You're tempted to say, "I told you so," or "You made your bed hard, now lie in it." But be reasonable! What good will this type of talk do for your relationship? It will destroy it. You may feel that you have valuable advice, but without a loving relationship your advice falls on deaf ears.

Who are the people you go to for advice? Are they the ones who constantly argue and belittle your decision, or are they the ones who love you and are ready to give a listening ear as well as a shoulder to lean on?

Yes, many young people are making messes of their lives. But remember the prodigal son's father? The wayward son went out and wasted his inheritance. When he ended up in the pig pen, he decided it was time to go home. I love the end of the story. When this son got within sight of his dad's place, he saw his dad looking down the road waiting for him to come home.

The father ran to his son and threw his arms around him. What a scene this must have been. If your child goes astray, will he find you waiting with open arms or will he find you with a finger pointing in his face?

Isaiah 53:6 teaches that we all have gone astray. Yet God is always ready to receive us again with open arms to restore us to the position of a son and an heir. Isn't this the least we can do for our children?

May God richly bless you as you reflect on what we have shared with you. Our job of raising children is ended. We are in the twilight years of enjoying being parents. We pray your life will be such that you can recommend it not only to your children but to your children's children. Remember it only takes a spark to get a fire going, but it takes a lot of fuel to keep the flame burning!

"Is not my word like fire? says the Lord," Jeremiah 23:29 (RSV). Fire burns away the dross and leaves the gold. Children are far more precious than fine gold. They have dross that needs to be burned away. The Word of God directs our paths as parents and gives us the proper value system for our children which brings out the gold in them.

In summary, successful parenting should not be measured by the way your children turn out. Children can choose to make the wrong choices even in a good environment. Our responsibility is to train them. What they do with our training is their choice. Strive to have a positive influence in their choices, but don't measure your success by the choices your children make. Being honorable, understanding you child, providing authority, giving supervision, offering positive options, disciplining and punishing correctly does not always guarantee a good end result in a child's life. But it does guarantee satisfaction in your heart and mind that your job was well done.

In II Kings 4 the story is told about a man of God who sees a Shunammite woman coming toward him. He sends his servant to greet her and ask, "Is it well with thee? Is it well with thy husband? Is it well with the child?"

She answers, "It is well."

If someone asked you the same question, how would you answer? Is it well with you, your husband and your child?

We hope as a Christian parent, who is learning and growing, you can answer with confidence, "Yes, it is well!"

References and Resources
Personality Type and Differences

Hirsh,S., and J.Kummerow. Lifetypes. NY: Warner Books,1989.
    A good book for understanding the basic differences in people.
    Examples and descriptions are easliy understood.

Keirsey,D.,and M.Bates. Please Understand Me. Del Mar,CA:
    Prometheus Nemesis Press,1984.
    A very popular book. The simple and useful vocabulary make it
    easy reading for the general public.

Lawrence,G. People Types and Tiger Stripes: A Practical Guide to
    Learning Styles. Gainesville, FL: Center for the Applications of
    Psychological Type,1979.
    Helpful in applying personality type concepts to education.

Myers,I. Gifts Differing. Palo Alto, CA: Consulting Psychologists
    Press,1980,1990.
    Describes type theory. Good examples but not recommended for
    those new to personality type and type theory.

If you cannot find these books through your local bookstore, then write to one of the following:

Consulting Psychologist Press
P.O. Box 10096
Palo Alto, CA 94303-0979

OR

CAPT
2720 N.W. 6th Street
Gainesville, FL 32609